NO King IN ISRAEL

THE HISTORY OF THE JUDGES

NO
King
IN ISRAEL
THE HISTORY OF THE JUDGES

Joel Portman

NO KING IN ISRAEL
By: Joel Portman
Copyright © 2008
GOSPEL FOLIO PRESS
All Rights Reserved

Published by
GOSPEL FOLIO PRESS
304 Killaly St. W.
Port Colborne, ON L3K 6A6
CANADA

ISBN: 978-1-897117-62-0

Cover design by Rachel Brooks

All Scripture quotations from the
King James Version unless otherwise noted.

Printed in USA

Contents

Foreword

No King in Israel will take the average person five hours to read. Years ago an older preacher remarked that some younger preachers had "bushels of words, but only spoonfuls of thought." However, in this book's pages you will find the very opposite, for it is pregnant with valuable thoughts. Mr. Portman commences his book with a general disposition of the Scriptures, giving us a spiritual x-ray of the divine structure of the Holy Writings. Not many books can be commended for this masterly approach. He then proceeds to descend to a lower altitude to have a closer look at prevailing conditions in the land during the era of the judges. Even delicate events, such as the Levite and his unfaithful concubine are meticulously investigated, followed by scriptural solutions that could have avoided that particular error. Not only this, but the many events related in this book are masterfully traced out and skillfully applied to relative conditions today. Even though the events exposed are ancient, yet the author applies the lessons that they afford to the assemblies of God's people today. This alone makes this publication exceedingly valuable. Linking the seven churches of Asia with people and events of the judges era is not only unique, but also a valuable lesson for us in this day of departure. This book is not "light reading," but is geared for the thoughtful and studious mind of a God-fearing saint. We highly commend the author for his skillful handling of divine truths, and recommend this book to all that love our Lord Jesus Christ.

—Robert E. Surgenor,
Brother and co-labourer

Preface

Theme and Pattern of the Book of Judges

The history of God's people, whether in the Old Testament or the New Testament, should always hold intense interest to us, upon whom *"the ends of the ages are come"* (1 Cor. 10:11, JND). God has given us this history so that we might learn from the examples of His dealings with Israel, His ancient people. His purpose is to cause us to heed and learn from their failures, so that their history will preserve us in our lives and service for Him. Neglecting to learn from their example and from God's way of bringing discipline against their sinful and rebellious failure will inevitably cause us to fall into the same trap and drift in the same direction. God's principles are unchanged and unchanging; therefore, it represents serious failure on our part to think that in this present day, often termed the "day of grace," He will wink at, or overlook, sin and departure. The reverse is more true to the Scripture. Since we possess more light and knowledge in this present dispensation, we also have greater responsibility and thus are more accountable for the character of our lives and service for Him.

We must approach a study of God's Word, or of any portion of it, in a manner that gives due seriousness to the text and teaching of Holy Scripture. We dare not force it into a mold formed from our own thinking or imaginative interpretation, but must consider it in its immediate context and in the light of all the revealed Word of God. Since Holy Scripture has come to us through *"holy men of God"* who wrote what the Holy Spirit originated and gave to them (2 Pet. 1:20), we recognize the solemnity of handling God's truth correctly. We purpose that our approach to this study of the book of Judges will take into ac-

9

count the literal truth that lies on the surface as it applies to the people of that period of time. We also desire to consider its typical interpretation in a way that ties it to other passages of God's Word. We believe that Old Testament passages and experiences also typically portray other periods of God's dealings, particularly the period of responsibility in which we live as believers in our Lord Jesus Christ during this "church age."

It is the author's contention (along with that of other respected commentators) that the events of this book of Judges typically and suggestively portray those different periods and conditions of the church age that are developed for us prophetically in Revelation 2-3. In saying that, it is obvious that the author takes the view that those chapters in Revelation give a historic outline of the church period. That is not to say that there are not other ways to study those chapters and apply their truths! We believe that they also contain practical teaching that applies to any assembly, even as the Lord of the churches directed those letters to existing assemblies of believers in John's day.

In this book, we will attempt to show the sequence in which these early books of our Bible develop and portray divine truth and how this remarkable book of history meshes with the books that precede and succeed it. We desire that all of us will appreciate the flow of God's Word, realizing that we should never separate any word, paragraph, chapter or book that God has given us from that which goes before and which comes after.

This book does not attempt to unravel the difficult historic chronology of Judges nor does it try to reconcile the differing accounting of the time periods that elapsed during this era. We refer to the statement in 1 Kings 6:1 and to Paul's mention of years in Acts 13:20. The issue of trying to decipher this chronology is very difficult when we consider the recorded periods during which each judge ruled Israel coupled with the fact that likely some of them were contemporaneous and ruled Israel in different parts of the country. For example, it seems clear from Judges 10:7 and 13:1, that Jephthah and Samson were contemporaries in their efforts against the foes of Israel. Jephthah opposed the Ammonites on the east of Jordan while Samson fought against the Philistines to the southwest.

If this is true, then it may also indicate that other judges were effectively delivering and leading God's people coincidentally, but in different areas of Israel. Other writers have written on this aspect of the book, and there are many and differing conclusions. Various attempts have been made to solve this puzzle. Some of the names of those books are listed in the bibliography at the end of this book along with references that any interested student can examine for himself. We have found Dr. Leon Wood's book, *Distressing Days of the Judges* (Zondervan, 1975), particularly valuable to understand the order of events. It is mainly from that book that we have tried to give some helpful information and have constructed the chart in the appendix that illustrates these events graphically. Dr. Woods also discusses the historical origins and characteristics of the oppressing and surrounding nations. The reader can examine those aspects of Judges from that book and others. However, for the most part, we will leave that aspect of the book to the "experts" and simply try to gain some spiritual insights through this study that apply to our needs regarding our service for the Lord today.

The subject of Judges is the theme of recurring periods of apostasy, or spiritual unfaithfulness and departure from the Lord, followed by a period of servitude to their enemies. This eventually caused their repentance and confession to the Lord. Upon this, God mercifully raised a deliverer and saved them. During the lifetime of the judge, they were maintained in a proper relationship with God and a period of peace ensued until his death. This cycle of departure–repentance–confession-deliverance-peace is not unusual; we see the same pattern in the history of the church period. We also acknowledge a similar cycle in our relationship with the Lord oftentimes. For this reason, the story of Israel in this case is intended to be a lesson for us so that we might be preserved by heeding their example.

We notice that the pattern of Judges is a sharp contrast with the events of Joshua. In the earlier book, Israel faithfully adheres to their God and is led in constant victory under their leader while in Judges, there is no constant leader and failure is more often the case. "Joshua is a picture of the potential of total victory that is available to every child of God, while Judges is a

11

picture of potential defeat which will be experienced every time one fails to totally drive out the enemy" (*King James Bible Commentary*). This pattern would substantiate the correspondence of these books with the events of Acts, in which the Spirit of God victoriously led His people to possess spiritual territory, but followed by subsequent failure in the history of the church age.

It does seem significant that the spiritual history of Israel anticipates and mirrors the spiritual history of the church. One can trace a coincidence between them starting with good beginnings based on the redemptive power of God to deliver. The pathway then continues by way of God's personal revelation of Himself, giving His Word to guide and control, and leading by His own power and wisdom. There is progress that results in possession of the inheritance that has been secured by God's power on their behalf. Other writers have noted this correspondence as well.

But we can also trace a corresponding decline in the response of the people. This decline in Israel and in the church is interrupted by times of revival and restoration, but it, in both cases, ultimately ends in degeneration, departure, and judgment from God. Along the way, God intervenes in discipline as He seeks to assert His control and to draw His people by His love. It is not without knowledge that the people of God degenerate; it is usually against knowledge and through expressing their self-will and rebellion against their God. This should make us fearful and concerned; it should move us to greater care and exercise, especially as we believe that we are moving toward the end of the present age during which God's dealings center on the church.

If Israel's history is any mirror of our own, it only indicates that the professing people of God increasingly wax colder and harder so that ultimately God's hand of discipline must fall on them. Paul reminds us, and we apply his words, *"Let him that thinketh he standeth, take heed lest he fall"* (1 Cor. 10:12). We also note that in the last letter of the Lord to the seven churches, Laodicea displays a spirit of self-satisfaction; even more, it shows an attitude of ignorance with regard to their true condition as the Lord sees and reveals it to be.

In sending this book out, we trust that the reader will receive spiritual help from the suggestions we have made in this book that are designed to guide, instruct and preserve each one of us from the same character of departure that was so manifestly seen in the history of Israel. Even though we have been regenerated and are indwelt by the Spirit of God, the human heart is still the same today, unchanged in us as well as in them. We do well to take heed, *"lest there be in any of you an evil heart of unbelief, in departing from the living God"* (Heb. 3:12). May God preserve us in fervent love for our blessed Lord, in fidelity to His glorious Person, and in faithfulness to His holy Word until the moment comes when He shall appear and we enter His presence for eternity!

In writing this book on Judges, the author has read every book he has had available in order to consider the views of other authors as much as possible. Every book has been examined with appreciation, for it is not the purpose of this book to negate the teaching that has gone before. *The Thirteen Judges* by A. M. S. Gooding contains much valuable material and help as also have the books by F. C. Jennings and by Samuel Ridout. Dr. Woods' book on Judges has been mentioned already and its helpful material has been taken into consideration. Reading these authors helps to balance and correct any mistakes that one might make in writing. However, as a result, it is possible that some authors have been quoted directly or indirectly without being acknowledged. Sometimes it seems impossible to sort out what might be original material and what has been "begged, borrowed, or stolen." Any direct or indirect quotation from another that has not been noted has not been done deliberately, and we sincerely apologize for such omissions. We would like to give all credit to other brethren who have written excellent books on this same portion of God's Word.

Appreciation is due those who gave help in making this book possible. Two good brethren, Mr. Jim Brown of Minneapolis, MN and Mr. Mark VanDerHart of Omaha, NE, both elders in their respective assemblies, have been especially helpful. They have carefully read the manuscript of the book as it was being written and have given me their thoughts, corrections and criticisms.

Assistance like this is invaluable and essential, and their help has been appreciated greatly. Others have also given help, including brother Robert Surgenor, who has encouraged and given comments along the way, and who has kindly consented to write a forward to the book. All these, as well as my patient wife, Janet, are very dear to me and important to the accomplishment of this work. May they receive their well-deserved reward from the Lord's hands!

Joel Portman
February 2008

1

Introduction

We believe that God has formed and ordered the worlds (ages) to accomplish and express His own purposes. James says, *"Known unto God are all His works from the beginning of the world"* (Acts 15:18). His creatorial work and the unfolding of the events of the ages have this intended purpose; this purpose includes, in large part, His attempt to teach men truths concerning Himself through the things that He has made (Ps. 19:1-4; Rom. 1:20; Heb. 11:3; Acts 17:24-27; Eph. 3:9-11). If we understand this blessed truth, it will enable us to see that He has designed every element of creation with its particular characteristic and habits so that they might serve His purpose to illustrate divine and spiritual truth.

In like manner, we also believe that He has ordered the events of history and has recorded those events in His precious Word to teach truths by way of principle, precept or pattern so we might be better able to comprehend more of His blessed ways. The Word of God has a depth and profundness to it exceeding our ability to grasp or comprehend, and we do well to appreciate its order that clearly indicates a divine author desiring to communicate His will and to reveal Himself to the sons of men.

Order of God's Word

Those who approach God's precious Word without appreciating its unity and uniqueness inevitably end up studying it as they would any other ancient book. Thus, they fail to receive edification or spiritual instruction by it, and they demean the spiritual and eternal purpose for which God has given it. As believers in the Lord Jesus Christ, we desire that our hearts, enlightened by the Holy Spirit and taught of Him, will appreciate the divine order even in the arrangement of events and the books, not only of the New Testament but also of the Old.

For example, one could discern an order in the arrangement of the epistles in the New Testament. In one sense, this order may be the result of man's arrangement, but perhaps we could agree that God seems to have superintended that arrangement for a purpose.

This order begins with Paul's great treatise on justification (Romans), which is the beginning and basis of our experience with God, and continues to develop further aspects of the corporate and individual life of the believer as a result of God's work, ending with an unfolding of the eternal future. Epistles that deal with assembly principles follow that basic book, and then those that may be termed epistles that are more of a "kingdom character" follow. Other orderings of books of our Bible clearly seem to reflect a sequence of divine development of truth revealed to men.

Order of Early Old Testament Books

It is valuable to discern a spiritual order in the early books of our Bible, beginning with Genesis and leading up to that part of the history that describes Solomon sitting on the throne of his glory and reigning over an expansive kingdom secured through the victories of his father, David.

Mr. A. M. S. Gooding has put it thus (*The Thirteen Judges*):

> "After the book of Judges, I repeat, there are the biographies of Saul, David and Solomon. Saul, the man of the flesh, the enemy of David, is removed in order that the warrior king David might establish the kingdom, and Solomon might sit upon the throne as the king of prosperity and peace. These three thus form a faint picture of events to take place after the church has been taken home.
>
> "I suggest therefore that the book [Judges] is applicable in teaching to the period from post-apostolic days until the rapture of the church."

Let us trace this order in a simple and brief way in order to see the position of Judges and its relation to God's movements toward His people. We may discern a dispensational order that gives us a picture of God's dealings with mankind through redemption through His own Son, the Lord Jesus Christ.

Dispensations?

We might only mention at this point that "dispensation" does not mean a certain, defined period of time, though it may include that aspect. It is rather an arrangement, or a manner of God's dealing with men, a set of certain conditions under which men were tried and under which God's purposes were developed. Mr. W. E. Vine says,

> "A 'dispensation' is not a period or epoch (a common, but erroneous, use of the word), but a mode of dealing, an arrangement, or administration of affairs."

There are some who reject a dispensational view of the Scriptures. However, without condemning any personally, we are convinced that the dispensational approach to the study of the Scriptures is more consistent and yields far greater riches to the student.

Samuel Ridout *(How to Study the Bible)* says,

> "By 'Dispensational Study,' we mean the study of the various ages, epochs, or dispensations into which the history of God's dealings with mankind from the beginning to the end of time are divided. Perhaps many Bible readers have never seriously thought of the self-evident fact that God has had different methods of dealing with men from the beginning to the present. Even where there is not entire ignorance as to this, the distinction between the dispensations has been but feebly grasped by the majority of God's people. Far be it from us for a moment to say that any portion of Scripture may not be profited by without this: but we fail in its full application and use unless we realize its setting."

Other writers could be quoted, along with the old and accepted statement regarding resolving difficulties in the Bible, "Distinguish the dispensations, and the difficulties will disappear."

Through this method of Bible study, we recognize God's progressive movements in His dealings with men and learn important truths from it.

Perhaps a brief consideration of the sequence of the early books of our Bible will help us place Judges in its proper position dispensationally. This may seem somewhat tedious, but it may also be helpful to prepare us to consider the teaching of this book. Let us notice the basic picture that each book presents to us.

Genesis

Without question, Genesis gives us the origin of truth, the first movements of God in his relationship with mankind, as well as the story of man's fall and disobedience to God. Genesis is often titled "The Way Down," and it certainly shows us the pathway of disobedience along with those results stemming from man's fall and sin's entrance into the Garden of Eden.

This book, standing at the portal of God's Word, begins by presenting a typical picture of man's creation, fall and redemption in chapters 1-2. Those chapters also teach us the origin of all things that have been created. It typically portrays the spiritual condition that resulted from a divine work that introduced life, a kind of life springing out of the midst of death and darkness. What a picture to us of what we (including all mankind) were by nature and in sin, separated from God in the darkness of our sinful state! However, we see the Spirit of God moving (Gen. 1:2) and manifesting His power to result in fruitfulness and a condition that God can enjoy in fellowship with mankind.

Genesis also shows us the origin of sin in the history of man. It teaches us the pathway of faith exhibited by the patriarchs, which Abraham primarily exemplified. We learn that what pleases God and gains one's acceptance before Him is believing Him (Gen. 15:6), a condition that stands in contrast to the unbelief that pervades the human heart. So we learn just what we are before God as sinners, and we also learn what God is looking for in the individual, "believing God." In addition, God gives us shadows of Christ and the cross in Genesis, especially when we study Isaac as the *"only son,"* and his being offered by Abraham in chapter 22. In Joseph we see our Lord Jesus Christ pictured in His rejection, His humiliation by His own brethren, and His ultimate exaltation to the throne. So Genesis is the "seed-plot" of Bible truths that are developed through the remainder of the book.

Exodus

In Exodus, God teaches us the way out of sin's bondage through the shedding and application of the blood of the unique Lamb. It is always God's plan and work to deliver His people from death, bondage and even out of Egypt itself. Exodus is "The Way Out," and it pictures the work of our great Redeemer to liberate us from sin's power and presence. Sadly, we also learn that they were out of Egypt, but Egypt and its influences were not out of them, a condition all too common among saints even today!

We learn at this point that God desires to have a redeemed people gathered to Himself to hear His voice and to be His peculiar (precious) treasure. He intends them to live in a covenant relationship with Him and He expects them to respond with desires to obey Him. In addition, we learn that those who He has redeemed will have ordered lives and movements in relation to His own dwelling place according to His commandment, for certainly the Tabernacle is a graphic picture to us of the local assembly of saints in the New Testament.

Leviticus

Having redeemed His people and arranged them in His own presence according to His will, God emphasizes that they are to be a holy priesthood, suitable for His holy presence and able to offer spiritual sacrifices (Heb. 13:15-16) to Him. Their lives are to be clean and set apart to Him (Lev. 11-16) and they are accepted and forgiven through the value of the person and work of the Lord Jesus (Lev. 1-7). Thus Leviticus is called "The Way In." God emphasizes that he also claims His people who have been redeemed by blood. As a result, our responsibility is to maintain lives conforming to His will and acknowledging His claims upon us.

Numbers

Having dealt with their relationship to God in Leviticus, Numbers shows us their relationship to the world. In the same way, 1 Peter 1:1-2:10 teaches us our link with the Lord who has saved us, and 1 Peter 2:11-5:13 seems to emphasize our relationship with the world in which we are *"strangers and pilgrims."* The same One who brought His people out of Egypt intended to bring them into the land, sustaining them all the way and holding out before them the beauty and fruitfulness of His purposes for them. Numbers shows us how God's people are on "The Way Through," and we move in the same way through a barren and desolate world in dependence on God to sustain us.

We appreciate in this book the grace and goodness of God expressing the development of His salvation and desires for His people. We learn that God never intended His people then (nor does He now) to settle down and to feel "at home" in a wilderness; this is how the child of God should see the present world.

It is a sad reflection on the quality of our profession as Christians if we are content with and occupied with the empty pleasures of this life, pursuing its aims and ambitions like those who are "earth dwellers." We are "in this world" but we are not of this world. Is not this the teaching of Galatians 1:4, *"deliver us from this present evil world* [age]*"*? Is it not also the expression of our Lord's heart in John 17:14-17 in His prayer for His people as their Great High Priest? We travel through, anticipating a better country (Heb. 11:13-16), and it is sad if we deny this truth by our manner of life.

Deuteronomy

In keeping with the title of the previous books, we can call Deuteronomy "The Way On," for it is occupied with fortifying and preserving saints so they will go on in the absence of their great leader. It seems that this book links itself with the last words of our blessed Lord to His own in the upper room before He went away (John 13-16). Deuteronomy is more than a reiteration of the law; it is an appeal from God as He seeks to reach the hearts of His own people, desiring more than their outward conformity to His Word. He mentions their heart 43 times in this book, and we learn the importance of obedience from the heart to preserve us in our spiritual pathway for God.

As Moses gives these last words to the people and then goes up and out of their sight for the last time, we think of the One who went away, up and out of the sight of His disciples. But before leaving them, He spoke tenderly to their hearts in His Upper Room ministry (John 13-17) so that they might be kept in the world and from evil (John 17:10-16). We follow those who were with Him on that occasion, and His precious Words have often encouraged and strengthened His saints to go on in faithfulness to our absent Lord.

Joshua

The departure of Moses, the lawgiver and deliverer, who could not bring them into the land, brings a new leader on the scene. Our Lord said to His own in John 16:7, *"it is expedient for you that I go away."* He was indicating the value of His departure in view of the coming of the Holy Spirit who would *"guide you into all truth"* (John 16:13) and who would institute the era, or dispensation, of the Holy Spirit of God on the Day of Pentecost. He was sent to lead the redeemed saints of God into the land that is often associated with the truth of Ephesians, the fullness of God's blessing for those who are *"seated with Christ in heavenly places"* (Eph. 1:3). It would seem that Joshua pictures to us the Holy Spirit. He led the people in victory after victory to possess the land, and then he divided it to them by lot for an inheritance. We, too, have an inheritance in Christ Jesus that is made real to us for our enjoyment through the work of the Spirit of God. It would be God's desire for His own people today that they too might possess the land and not fail to go in to enjoy what is so precious to Him who is our God.

It is important to notice that the promised inheritance in the land could not be actually possessed except by conquest of the occupying nations. We learn that it is through personal exercise and effort to overcome opposing foes in spiritual places that we are able to enjoy those blessings associated with our position in Christ. Joshua divided the inheritance of the land to the 12 tribes of Israel so that their portion in the land was determined by God's choice for them. However, we learn very quickly that the ancient dwellers of the land were determined to hinder their progress and prevent them from possessing it. That truth has its clear application to the early days of church history as well as today, individually, with regard to the believer's life and blessings.

Judges

Now, having come to Judges, we can see that it follows the sequence of previous books. Deuteronomy suggested to us the last words of our Lord prior to His return to glory, then Joshua indicated our position in Christ in heavenlies, and now we see in Judges the experience of God's people after the apostles were removed from this scene.

In this book, we learn the necessity for divine leadership among God's people after those who, like Joshua, having extraordinary power from God, are taken from the scene. The issue then and now is, "Who will rise to the standard and carry on that work with faithfulness?" We find this call reechoed by Paul in his last epistle to Timothy. He was not only concerned with Timothy's faithfulness in service, but also about the urgency of identifying those who would faithfully follow him (2 Tim. 2:1-2).

Judges is a sad record of failure following the initial victories of the first chapter. However, even those early victories were mingled with failure, and later failures were mingled with victories under the judges, an indication of what has marked church testimony from the beginning in the book of Acts. As F. C. Jennings suggests in his book on Judges, "It is a record of events so written, as not only to be faithful history, but pictorial prophecy." It exemplifies the truth of 1 Corinthians 10:11, that those things that are written, which happened to them, are written for our learning. If we fail to learn from their example, then we are certainly doomed to follow the same pathway.

With regard to this view, F. W. Grant writes,

"For us the typical application is but too plain. If Joshua has shown us the portion and blessing of a heavenly people, Judges gives us without any doubt the history of that people. The church visible is here seen in its decline and corruption, its broken condition and captivity for its sins to different forms of error and evil, along with God's way of deliverance from these exemplified in many partial deliverances. The coming of the Lord, the only complete and final deliverance, could not, of course, be pictured here" (*Numerical Bible*).

Again, A. M. S. Gooding, in his book *The Thirteen Judges*, says,

"The truth connected with them [the 13 judges] will be best applied in the period commencing about two generations after the descent of the Spirit of God and the commencement of the church period, in other words, the post-apostolic period; similar to that brought before us in Revelation 2 and 3 in the letters to the seven churches of Asia… I suggest therefore that the book is applicable in teaching to the period from post-apostolic days until the rapture of the church."

A careful study of Judges reveals that the events of the book are not in strict chronological order. Some of the judges worked contemporaneously and the last events of the book actually occurred near the beginning of the book. (See Appendix I for a suggested chronology of the book). However, the sequence of events in the book suggests that the Spirit of God has ordered this presentation for a purpose. We suggest that its purpose is that it might present a pictorial view of the church age and God's on-going acts to preserve His people.

The course of this book is a record of departure, with God repeatedly intervening to raise up men to recover and deliver His wandering, wayward people. Since God's desire is always to bless His own, those men who judged Israel represented His grace, mercy and longsuffering with them. He was not willing that their testimony or history would end with such failure, thus he raised men to act on His behalf to restore and liberate them from the results of their sinfulness. This history is summarized for us in Judges 2:6-23. *"It repented the Lord because of their groanings by reason of them that oppressed them and vexed them"* (v. 18). As always, He acted in mercy toward them, and the judges acted for God to deliver and preserve His people. Paul emphasizes this in Acts 13:20 as also does the psalmist in Psalm 106:34-47.

In the same way, during the age of church history from Pentecost to the rapture of the church, God has repeatedly moved to recover His saints from the results of their own ways. Yet He also traces, in Revelation 2-3, the downward trend that reflects the pattern seen in Judges, ending in a Laodicean condition where *"every man did that which was right in his own eyes"* (Judg. 21:25). It is delightful to see that even in such degenerating days, there were those who remained faithful; we admire those such as Boaz (Ruth 2), who emerged from a famine as a *"mighty man of wealth"* in contrast to Elimelech and his disastrous choice.

Ruth

This lovely, short book centers on the recovery of a desolate widow (Naomi) who has moved far from the place of God's choice to lose all in a Gentile land. This sad story is followed by her being blessed in connection with a Gentile bride being married to a mighty man of wealth (Boaz). It is not difficult to see this as a picture of the marriage of the church, the Gentile bride of Christ, to Him who also will work to restore Israel to her place, a place far better than what she has lost.

This anticipates the glorious future for Israel that God speaks of repeatedly in His Word, a future restoration that will be linked with the glory of Christ united with His blood-bought bride, the church. It looks forward to the day following the period of church testimony that will begin with the rapture of the church and God's resumption of dealings with His earthly people once again. It is precious to see that the end of Ruth clearly links this event with the coming of the great warrior King of whom David is a picture. We look for that long-awaited day and thank God for the nearness of that event that will bring us to Him eternally.

Ruth also depicts for us the tremendous loss that results from leaving the place where God has put us and where He has promised to bless us. Elimelech likely thought that he would prosper in Moab (a picture of the world system around us), but instead, he lost everything in that strange land. Boaz is a contrast; he was a man who stayed where He knew the Lord had divided him an inheritance, and in that place he prospered and was a channel of blessing to others as well as the means of restoration of Elimelech's family after the few of them returned. No doubt Boaz also pictures the Lord, as we noted above, but he also typifies a faithful child of God who is not easily influenced by difficult conditions that may come on God's people.

1 Samuel – 2 Samuel

All these events culminate with the crowning of the king of peace who ruled over the largest expanse of Israelite territory. David's conquering and Solomon's pacific reign were preceded by that of a king who was the people's choice, permitted by God to occupy the throne. Leaving aside the question of whether Saul was a true believer or not, we see in him a typical presentation of a man who pleased the people but who was a constant impediment to the ascension of the rightful king to the throne. In this way, Saul suggests the Antichrist.

David projects our minds forward to the coming of our Lord Jesus in power and glory, defeating all His foes and subduing all the nations under His power (Zech. 12:1-9; 14:1-11). That event will then lead into the peaceful and prosperous reign, pictured by the reign of Solomon, that will be His for the duration of the millennium and into eternity. His victory will usher in the kingdom reign and glory of our Lord Jesus Christ when we, as His people, shall reign with Him and enjoy the fruits of His toil and suffering.

Until then, we act in our present responsibility as we recognize that our service for Him in this period of His rejection will determine our position with Him in the day of His glory. Again, quoting A. M. S. Gooding, "These three [Saul, David, Solomon] form a faint picture of events to take place after the church has been taken home."

Dispensational Order

All these books indicate to us a dispensational order that God has given by means of their arrangement. Beginning with the darkness and disorder that characterized us and this world in the confusion of sin, it ends at this point with an ordered government, with the rightful king ruling, and peace pervading the entire kingdom. As such, we can see that the book of Judges, picturing the present period and God's manner of dealing with men in this age of the church, represents an integral part of the God's purpose in view of attaining that goal.

This should emphasize to us the importance of our responsibility to uphold the testimony to the name of our departed, absent Lord until He comes. While the surrounding world has degenerated religiously and is degenerating further, God is always calling a remnant to remain faithful, to maintain His principles until the end of our days. Zechariah exhorted the people in his prophecy, *"For who hath despised the day of small things?"* (4:10). Nothing can be small or insignificant if it is part of God's on-going purpose regarding His house and the testimony to His name. Israel might well have felt a measure of sorrow for the weak and lowly state in which they were found at that point of recovery. However, the point is that it was a work of God and because it was, what He was doing was not to be measured in terms of size or grandeur. It was to be seen in relation to the furtherance of His work in that day, and it was a call for their fervent response to His call to work and their faithful adherence to His command. We do well to respond in like manner as they did, when we think of the privileged part He has allowed us to have to maintain something that is for His honour and eternal praise.

2

Similarities Between
Judges and the Church Age

A study of the book of Judges in relation to the letters to the seven churches and the characteristics of the church age indicates a correspondence that we can observe between the two. We will summarize briefly some of those relationships and then develop them further in our analysis of the book.

Their Good Beginning

First, we see that in both cases, God's people began well. However, even with their good beginning, there were the seeds of ultimate failure to be found among them and seen in their actions. This good beginning, for Israel, was based on their being in a right position, possessing the land and enjoying that inheritance that had been secured for them. They were enjoying the fruits of the faithfulness and ability of Joshua as described in the previous book.

We find that this was true of the church in Acts. The believers were established in the truth of God, having come out by being separated from identification either with Judaism, or with their past pagan associations. The Holy Spirit had opened to their view the panorama of truth concerning all that was theirs in Christ. By the teaching of the apostles (Acts 2:43; 13:1) they were being fed the truths given by the Holy Spirit of God. More truth was to be unfolded to their understanding as God gave gift to local assemblies and gifted men to the church (1 Cor. 13:9-12; Eph. 4:9-17). Just like Israel in the land, they began to enjoy the plenitude that God had intended for them in their redemption.

Writing to the assembly in Ephesus, the Lord calls attention to their knowledge of truth by which they had tested those who proved to be false (Rev. 2:2-3). That knowledge was coupled with their works, labor and patience, so it was proven in reality of life and conduct. Thus we see that a similarity exists between the initial position and beginning of both Israel and the early church.

Early Zeal and Desire for Progress

Then, we note that immediately they displayed zeal and a desire to move forward through conflict to possess more fully the inheritance that was theirs. In Judges, Judah took the lead to exercise the rightful authority that the Lord had entrusted to that tribe. This was an authority and leadership that is linked with Christ (Gen. 49:10). As they began the work to conquer the foe, they depended on God to lead and give the needed power, and we see that the Lord worked on their behalf and delivered the Canaanites and Perizzites into their hand (Judg. 1:4). In addition, the people displayed a desire to move forward in fellowship with their brethren (Judg. 1:3, 17), a characteristic that we also observe in the early church activities. This good beginning should continue to characterize us in our activities and service for God today; self-sufficiency and independence from our brethren is not a good thing and usually demonstrates a spirit that is opposed to God's principles.

Early Indications of Failure

Next, however, we cannot help observing the early development of failure. Contradicting what we have said in the previous paragraph, perhaps the dependence of Judah on Simeon indicated a lack of confidence in God. Their inclusion can be justified by knowing the close relationship their territories had (Simeon's possession actually lay within that of Judah, Joshua 19:1). Nevertheless, it was an indication of Judah's failure when they depended on Simeon for success in the battle rather than to depend wholly on God. God had told Judah to go up but had said nothing about Simeon.

This also suggests a constant problem in Christian testimony and service; there often seems to be an inability to depend unreservedly and confidently on the power of God to accomplish His work. Fellowship in work is good and commendable, but a fine line exists between that fellowship and an unwillingness to place complete confidence in the Lord. In addition, we observe that, from the outset, they failed to drive out the former possessors of the land (Judg. 1:19, 21, 27, etc.). They were only partially victorious, though God had commanded them to drive them **all** out of the land. God knew the dangers of those nations remaining in the land and it was for their preservation as a nation that He commanded to destroy and drive them out. As a result of their failure, Israel lost their separation and mingled themselves among the people (Judg. 1:21, 27, 29, 30, etc.). This inevitably led to more weakness, and ultimately, to their downfall.

We see the same pattern emerging in this period of the church. Initial separation and judgment of evil associations soon gave way to compromise and intermingling with the unsaved. This was the characteristic of some in Corinth (1 Cor. 10) and also seems to have been true of other gatherings. We especially see it in the case of Pergamos in Revelation 2, where the church joined hand in hand to walk with the world, enjoying a closeness to the world that resulted in distance from the Lord.

These seven major nations of Judges (Deut. 7:1) may have seemed overwhelming due to their power, but that was because Israel had gotten their eye off God. Of course, they could make many excuses, such as the enemy having greater weapons and chariots of iron (Josh. 17:14-18; Judg. 1:19). Excuses only indicate unbelief operating in the hearts of God's people. Early on, they had left their "first love." The nations also became attractive to them, so that they learned and practiced their ways, including their religious customs. It is not difficult to see the same pattern emerging in the church period, and inevitably, this is always the result of a breakdown of separation by God's people. The nations of Canaan represent spiritual powers that are hostile to God's people, both internal and external powers that work to prevent blessing and fruitfulness through faithfulness to the Lord.

Development of Failure

We notice that as time progressed in Israel's history in Judges, as well as in that of the churches, the enemy's power seemed to increase. Servitude to the nations was generally for longer periods of time as the book progresses. This was, in large part, due to their increasing sinfulness and distance from God. We can see this trend generally suggested from the chart below:

Nation in Power		Years of Servitude
Mesopotamia	(3:8)	8
Moab	(3:14)	18
Canaan	(4:3)	20
Midian	(6:1)	7
Ammon, Philistines	(10:7)	18
Philistines	(13:1)	40

From this, we see that as time progressed, the power of the people of God **seemed** to decrease while the power of the enemy increased. Without doubt, we can see the same pattern displayed in the church age, with less power to overcome and progress spiritually now than there was in the past. That pattern marked the first 2-300 years of the church, especially upon the apostles' passing and the death of those who immediately followed them. It follows the example of Israel in Judges 2:10, when, with subsequent generations, there eventually *"arose another generation after them, which knew not the Lord, nor the works which He had done for Israel."*

Not only were there generally longer periods of servitude in Judges, but it is remarkable that their expressed desire for deliverance gradually decreased. In Judges 2:4, the people wept when the angel of the Lord came to Bochim and reproved them. This is the only time we read that they wept before the Lord until chapter 20:23, 26 when their brother-tribe Benjamin defeated them on two occasions and later when they had nearly annihilated Benjamin. So we learn that there was decreasing sensitivity to God's voice, and a sad lack of self-judgment with repentance, a condition that is not unknown in our day as well.

In addition, in Judges 3:9, 15; 4:3; 6:6; 10:10 (5 times) they cried to the Lord for deliverance from enemy domination. In chapter 6:10, they didn't respond to God's warning but, even worse, in chapter 13:1 there is no cry for deliverance at all. They were satisfied to remain under Philistine bondage. Moreover, in chapter 15:11, they were quite ready to deliver Samson into the hands of the Philistines rather than to support him in his work against the enemy! This only indicates a weakening condition that eventually resulted in their being content to submit to God's enemies rather than depend on the Lord and move in faithfulness to Him and His Word.

Likewise in the church age, we see a similar spiritual state in which the elements of the spiritual powers of this world have so influenced what is called "Christian testimony" that in some cases it is hard to discern what is truly of God and what is of the world!

Less Spiritual Judges

Along with this condition of placid acceptance, we note that the judges that God raised to deliver and rule His people were progressively less spiritual as the book moves forward. It can be noted that from Othniel to Ehud there is a decline, though not so marked as that from Ehud to Barak, who was a man who refused to obey God without Deborah going with him to battle (Judg. 4:8)! From Gideon to Jephthah we see a further decline. The character of the two men is a contrast: Gideon was occupied with threshing wheat to get food for himself and the people during a time of adversity, but Jephthah had been expelled by his brethren and lived with vain men. In addition, Gideon responded directly to God's call to deliver Israel without any pre-conditions, but Jephthah was called by the people and only served after bargaining with them (Judg. 11:7-10). We could mark other contrasts by means of a study of these two men, such as their character following the victory: Gideon appeased his brethren with soft words (8:1-3) and refused to rule over the people while Jephthah killed his opposing brethren (12:1-6) and wanted a place of prominence.

If there is a contrast between these two judges, we note that the difference between Jephthah (including all the preceding judges) and Samson is vast. In Samson we find a man who had the most natural ability, the most power, the most "gift" from God, but coupled with the most carnality, self-centeredness and complete lack of any genuine spiritual exercise to deliver Israel. For example, we see a man who never prayed except for his own deliverance from his enemies (Judg. 15:18; 16:28). In addition, he mainly exercised his great power to accomplish his own desires for vengeance or for personal gain. He represents the sad decline and spiritual departure seen so evidently today that has been marked over the course of the church age.

We also can say that this decline seen in the judges only reflected the continuous spiritual decline of the people from which they arose and who God had called them to lead. They were the product of their day, some better, but others much the same. This is also true of those who function as leaders among the saints of the church age; they cannot be separated from the milieu of believers with which they are associated and from which they come. If there is weakness among the saints, there also will be that same weakness reflected in those who are their leaders. In addition, weakness in the leaders will produce weakness in the saints.

The End Condition

Finally, at the end of Judges, we see complete indifference to spiritual departure among them as evidenced by Micah and his house of idols that he built (17:1-6). We recognize that these chapters describe events that took place historically much earlier in the book. If these events took place earlier in Israel's history, what must their condition have been at the end of the period of the Judges? These chapters have been placed here for a definite purpose. God is showing that this will be the marked characteristic at the end of this church age. Israel could tolerate this kind of evil among them at this point without any objection.

However, following that sad but accepted condition, we note the moral degeneration that inevitably follows spiritual evil (Judg. 19). It is most interesting that while the spiritual, idolatrous evil was not condemned, the nation was extremely severe in judging the moral results that flowed from it so that they virtually exterminated a tribe of Israel! Is this not the case with Christendom? Elements of Babylonish religion are accepted and incorporated into "Christian" worship, even while there may be abhorrence of moral evil. However, since *every man did that which was right in his own eyes,* inevitably moral depravity will enter in and cause great ruin to the entire testimony that God intends to be sacred for Himself.

As in Romans 1, spiritual declension and rejection of what God has revealed concerning Himself will always lead to further degeneration in man's moral climate. This makes clear that men cannot reform or maintain a right moral condition when they reject God and ignore His truth. This is the present case and condition of the religious world in which we live near the end of this age. May God preserve us in a discerning and separated walk, seeking to please Him in all we do or say.

Where are We?

If we were to identify ourselves with any particular condition depicted in Judges, where would we place ourselves? We hope that we could relate to those who faithfully sought to uphold God's truth and deliver the people. It is obvious, though, that in general we are in the midst of those conditions depicted in the last part of the book. Sadly, it seems clear that increasingly most everyone is inclined toward doing what is right in his own eyes and is not seeking the mind of God for guidance. It is easy to look at difficulties that exist and then devise means that seem right to deal with those problems. However, it may be that those innovative changes are only an expression of this characteristic, and the end result will be worse than the problem at the first. There is great need today for recovery to the truth of God, even among those who profess to be gathered alone to the name of our Lord Jesus Christ in simple assembly testimony. May God work to this end for the preservation of such gatherings for His own name's sake!

We would hope that these features and their resemblance to church age characteristics will become clearer as we proceed. We do not intend to excessively force the picture on the passage or go far beyond what is written. We only make the comparison and suggestions that we see at times as shadows but not clearly. However, there is much in this book that we can learn about the day in which God has called us to maintain responsible testimony for Him. We will have to answer to Him when our day of service is over. May God teach us some things through this book that would preserve us in our pathway for our blessed Lord.

3

Brief Summary of Major Periods of Judges

At this point, it would be helpful to mark out the major periods of the book of Judges and the experience of God's people. The book divides into three sections as Dr. Leon Woods indicates in his book, *Distressing Days of the Judges*. The first division is from 1:1-3:6, and this deals with their failure to possess the land and summarizes their condition religiously. The second division, 3:7-16:31, records the history and exploits of the judges along with the intervening periods of sin and degeneration of the people. The last division, Judges 17:1-21:25, gives two stories that illustrate the conditions that existed through the entire period of the judges. These conditions caused the recurrence of their times of discipline under God's chastening hand.

In keeping with our purpose to relate this book to the events of the church age, we will divide the book into other parts that help to delineate the typical relationship that exists between these periods and the seven churches and their characteristics in Revelation 2-3. We will note that there were six periods of servitude that came between seven phases when major judges ruled to deliver the people. These periods are marked each time by the repeated expression; the children of Israel *"did evil in the sight of the Lord"* (2:11; 3:7, 12; 4:1; 6:1; 10:6; 13:1). The domination by an enemy was the direct result of their departure from the Lord, an act that was evil in the Lord's sight, regardless of how they expressed it in moral conditions. Such departure, for us as well as for those addressed by the Lord in Revelation 2-3, is the root of the evil conditions that follow. Faithful practices and moral lives cannot exist without close adherence to the Lord and fidelity to His Word.

We can link those periods under their different conditions with the enemies and servitude that followed, to divide the book into essentially seven sections that roughly correspond with the periods of church history. Each judge that God raised up was a deliverer from the particular enemy that preceded him, as follows:

Church Period	Phase/ Judge	Enemy
EPHESUS	**Beginning** (ch. 1-2) Marked by a good start, but with failure to go on well and maintain the conflict to possess the land. Ch. 2:1 reveals the problem...they had left their first love for God. Mingling among their enemies resulted with unfaithfulness to God. This resulted in their servitude to Mesopotamia.	**Mesopotamia** Place where Abraham was when God called him...represents the attraction of the former life and natural affections. World allowed in life resulting in its control.
SMYRNA	**Othniel** (ch. 3:1-11) Deliverance of people being sustained in persecution through the encouraging Word of God at the right time. Overcoming through weakness yet in the power of God working through His Word. This was followed by domination of Israel by Moab.	**Moab (Eglon)** Pride of man and desire for self-exaltation of the flesh. Self-indulgence seen and desire for comfort. This condition led to Ehud.
PERGAMOS	**Ehud** (ch. 3:12-30) Delivered from Moab's persecution and oppression through union with the world resulting in its favour.	**Canaan** Materialism, commercial activity, prosperity. All promoted in Pergamos and became a bondage.

BRIEF SUMMARY OF MAJOR PERIODS OF JUDGES

Church Period	Phase/ Judge	Enemy
THYATIRA	**Deborah/Barak** (ch. 4:1-5:31) Characterized by a woman in authority. Victory over Canaan accomplished by a woman (Jael) living in pilgrim character, driving the tent peg through the temples, the source of wrong thoughts and ambitions. Yet men, who God intended to lead, are seen in Barak to be weak and unable to take responsibility to act for God.	**Midian/Amalek** Contention caused by power of a kindred people marked by strife and contention to rob God's people of blessing, resulting in spiritual impoverishment.
SARDIS	**Gideon** (ch. 6:1-8:35) Name means "cutter down" and suggests the reformation period and recovery. Followed by rule of a man not raised up of God who dominated God's people (Abimelech), yet Jotham represents a faithful remnant during this period.	**Ammon and Philistines also** Self-will and human wisdom exercised. The result of a walk without faith as Lot. Sardis had a "name to live, but thou art dead."
PHILADELPHIA	**Jephthah** (ch. 11:1-12:7) Man humbled and despised and with much weakness. Could not reconcile or unite God's people. Fighting between Israelites as people of God.	**Philistines** Religious people professing salvation, living in the land but not with the same call as Israel. Element of a different character than others; was not one of the nations they were to destroy upon entering the land.
LAODICEA	**Samson** (ch. 13:1-21:25) A deliverer marked by self-will, doing what pleased him. People satisfied with Philistine domination. Moral decay and spiritual departure evident. God's people actually worse than men of the world. Resulted in last conditions described with spiritual idolatry and moral evil that was caused by every man doing that which was right in his own eyes.	

These are not intended to suggest absolutely clear similarities between the events of Judges and the church age. However, the same could be said about other typical pictures of the church age such as the parables of the kingdom in Matthew 13, the sequence of kings of Judah and Israel, and other typical relationships that have been drawn. These are presented so that we might learn some of the underlying principles and patterns that have also been unfolded in the dispensation of the church. We also need to learn lessons that apply to our lives and to assembly practices in our day.

May God help us to learn something from this book of Judges that may help us to recognize the need for faithful perseverance in our lives personally and in assembly testimony generally in view of His coming and our being gathered together unto Him (2 Thess. 2:2).

4

Early Departure and Reproof by an Angel
Ephesus and Leaving First Love
First Enemy: Mesopotamia

Judges opens with a description of new conditions that had never before existed in Israel. Prior to this point, they had leaders such as Moses and Joshua who God had clearly raised up to deliver them from their enemies and to give them divine guidance. Now, after the death of Joshua (Judg. 1:1), God expected them to seek guidance directly from Him. They began by doing so, and if they had continued to do so, they would not have ended by doing what was right in their own eyes (Judg. 21:25). Even though there was no king in Israel, God never intended to leave them with no source for divine authority or means of giving clear direction to His people.

Why the Judges?

In our study of this book, it helps when we understand why the events of this book follow the possession of the land rather than God immediately giving the people a king. We need to understand that God's ideal government for His people (and eventually for the universe) is a theocracy, which is a form of government in which God personally controls His world. That form of control is what He also desires in any local assembly; it is the rule of heaven through the men that He has raised up in that assembly (Matt. 18:18). In the beginning He exercised that control through a man when God instituted a man to rule over creation (Adam, Ps. 8:3-8; Heb. 2:5-8) but God always intends that man will rule as a representative of God. Through Adam's disobedience, he fell and all creation fell with him, but God's initial purpose is still His ultimate purpose. He will have a man who will rule directly under His authority, and that Man will be Christ.

For them to look to God directly for their guidance (through the priesthood) would result in His people acknowledging His supreme position of authority. When they failed to do so, due to their sin and departure, God raised up the men as judges who acted to deliver them and to lead them back to a right relationship with God. The element that ruined God's purpose in this way was their sin that came between them and God. They continually departed from allegiance to God and turned after false gods of the nations around them.

A Monarchy

As time went on in this book, we see that the departure and rejection of God's authority increased so that eventually, God allowed them a king and raised up David to sit on the throne. A monarchical form of government, as ultimately resulted in Israel, was farther removed from that under which God initially tested His people. It was farther removed from a theocracy. For one thing, it involved a man who continued to rule until he died, whether he was good or evil. Instead of a temporary work as that which the judges accomplished to answer a particular condition, theirs was a permanent position that could continue regardless of the results.

This is not to say that God could not nor did not remove wicked kings, for example, Ahab and Manasseh. A true theocracy knows no earthly king at all. Only if the king actively sought guidance from God and acted accordingly would it approximate divine rule over God's people. Saul was rejected by God from being king over Israel for the fundamental reason that he disobeyed the commandment of the Lord (three times we read that God rejected him in 1 Samuel 15:23, 26; 16:1 and in each case it is because Saul rejected the word of the Lord). David was likely the king that came closest to fulfilling that ideal in that he was a *"man after God's own heart"* and sought to obey the Lord. It is noteworthy that the kings that followed David on the throne of Judah were compared with him, whether or not they walked in his ways.

Dr. Leon Woods, in his book *Distressing Days of the Judges*, has stated the differences well and we give a partial quotation from that book:

> "The form of rule substituted [a monarchy] was not only a "second-best" from God's viewpoint, but also from the people's viewpoint, and this in two respects. The first concerns the matter of potential blessings and consequent advertisement for God... They would have enjoyed the finest blessing under this 'best' form of rule...Second, this change of government called for heavy taxation of the people. Under God's 'best' form, there had been no need of taxes to support a civil government. There was no king or expensive court, no civil programs or authorities; the people could live tax free...God's instruction to Samuel... is noteworthy. God told him to accept the request but to warn the people that this change would come; the king they would get would make severe demands of taxation upon them (1 Sam. 8:9-18)."

The judges were not elected by the people, nor was judgeship a hereditary position (as was kingship). They were not official men in the same sense as the kings were. We notice that Gideon, when offered the position as king with his sons to follow him (Judg. 8:22-23), rejected their request with the response, *"the Lord shall rule over you."* Evidently, Gideon recognized the principle of a theocracy among the people. It is sad that one of his sons (by a concubine) was only too eager to take the position that his father had rejected. The leadership of the judges depended on the people recognizing that God had raised them for that purpose. It also depended on the quality of their leadership and their ability to bring about deliverance of the people from their oppressors. They were men who gave evidence that God had raised them for that purpose, in that they came to that place at a time when the people were ready to accept their leadership accompanied by the evidences of spiritual ability (usually, though not in all cases of the judges). Their work was an extension of God's rule over His people and expressed His desire to bring them back to Himself.

Who were the Judges?

The word that is translated "judges" is one that indicates "one who leads, or judges" among the people. The first mention of judges among Israel is in Numbers 25:5, *"And Moses said unto the judges of Israel, Slay ye every one his men that were joined unto Baal-peor."* So judges existed prior to this period of time, and they evidently refer to men who had a position of leadership under Moses (Ex. 18:21-22, 25-26).

Those who are called judges in this book were also those who were "saviours" (deliverers) of the people. In Acts 13, Paul recounts the history of Israel in the synagogue at Antioch in Pisidia, and the judges are listed in the context of those that God raised up as saviours of His people. We see in this book the work of deliverance was the first work they undertook, followed (in some cases) by judging the people and maintaining right conditions for God. Samson as a judge would be an exception to that; it is never recorded that he actually judged Israel though he fought against their enemies.

There were a total of fourteen judges including Eli and Samuel, both of whom judged Israel prior to the days of the kings and during the period of the judges. To these could be added the two sons of Samuel (Joel and Abiah, 1 Sam. 8:2). However, God did not raise these up, but they were appointed by their father and they failed to rise to the same standard of character that marked the others. We omit Abimelech, of course, since he was not raised up of God, neither did he present any spiritual or delivering qualities that would qualify him for any position among the judges. His was a position of domination maintained by force and cruelty.

Of these fourteen, only twelve are listed in the book of Judges. Out of this total, six are generally considered to be "major" and the remainder were "minor." That distinction primarily depends on the relative space devoted to the history of each judge and the extent of their judgeship. In the case of the "major" judges (Othniel, Ehud, Deborah/Barak, Gideon, Jephthah, Samson), they were also those who effectively delivered the people from oppression, while the minor judges, apart from Shamgar, are not so listed. The other relatively "minor" judges include Tola (10:1), Jair (10:3), Ibzan (12:8), Elon (12:11), and Abdon (12:13).

We conclude that the leadership role of these men was two-fold: in the first place, they were called of God to deliver His people from oppression as an expression of His mercy toward them (Judg. 2:16). The word used in most cases is that they "delivered" the people, or "saved" them. Secondly, they also functioned as judges who ruled for God for the period during which they were alive following their victory.

This two-fold role would also relate to the men that God raises up over His people as spiritual leaders in a local assembly. They are called upon to deliver God's people from every oppressing form of bondage and they are to lead the people under God's authority. This always results, when properly exercised, in a period of rest for the saints (Judg. 3:11, 30; 5:31).

Difficulty of Allowing God to Lead

It is much more difficult to seek God's mind directly and wait on Him for guidance than it is to follow human leadership. Is that at least part of the reason why men have risen to prominence in the church age, even from the earliest days? Paul predicted to the Ephesian elders in Miletus that *"also of your own selves shall men arise, speaking perverse things, to draw away disciples after them"* (Acts 20:30). It was not long before that actually took place, as we read in church history when ecclesiastical positions and orders began to be sought after and practiced very early after the death of the apostles. We find that even those who had known the apostles and survived them began accepting positions of authority over groups of churches contrary to what those apostles had taught.

Miller writes (*Church History*),

> "Scarcely had the voice of inspiration become silent in the church, than we hear the voice of the new teachers crying loudly and earnestly for the highest honors being paid to the bishop, and a supreme place being given to him. This is evident from the Epistles of Ignatius, said to have been written A. D. 107."

Along with this, a distinction between the "clergy" and the "laity" began to be made, a distinction that only deepened and solidified over time. This has resulted in the plethora of denominations today, as men have followed human leaders into dividing one from another (1 Cor. 1:12). Such a sad state has its beginnings in the example established by those who followed former men of God.

Seeking God's Guidance

We do see an exercise to know the will of God at the beginning of this book (ch. 1:1). However, it is also interesting that we do not read this or similar expressions in the book until the end (ch. 20:18, 27), during the battle with their own brother Benjamin. Was this the root cause of the prevalent problems during this time? Not seeking to know and obey the will of God will always result in spiritual departure and degeneration in life and testimony. Had Israel sought and followed God's will, continuing to move in fellowship with God and one another, they would have been preserved from the sorrows and servitude that resulted.

And in the church age, had men sought God's will by simply studying and obeying God's Word, adding nothing to or taking nothing from it, they would have been preserved from instituting ecclesiastical practices or establishing organizational systems in local churches or among groups of churches. The majority of the outward expressions of religious practices in churches today are only the result of men **not** seeking to know and follow the clear guidance of God's Word. The Lord Jesus said *"If a man will do his will, he shall know of the doctrine…"* (John 7:17). This is always the preservative for God's people, now as well as then.

Enemies Surrounding

Israel was surrounded by enemies, the original inhabitants of the land and those around it. These seven nations, along with the others, represent spiritual principles that always seek to inhibit and prevent the progress of God's people. It is notable that in 1 Kings 11, we find that Solomon was led astray from his first love by his involvement with wives from the nations surrounding them. These nations were not those of the Canaanites, but they were those from the nations on the borders of Israel. As such, though he might have thought that they were not of the same category as the forbidden ones, yet God records that He had told them not to do this thing. It seems to represent an attempt on his part to compromise divinely-given principles and to circumvent the prohibition of God's Word, but it led to his downfall. We are told in Ephesians 6:10 that we are in the midst of a warfare, even though seated with Christ in the heavenlies. Wherever there are divinely-granted possessions to inherit, there will also be opposing elements that will do everything possible to prevent the people of God from enjoying them. One could suggest different spiritual identities of these nations, and perhaps that will become clear as we look at them individually.

God said in Judges 2:3; 3:1-4 that He would not drive these nations out before them due to their disobedience. He left them so that these nations might prove Israel's faithfulness to His Word and so that each generation might learn how to fight the foe. We read in Exodus 17:16 that the Lord swore that He would have war with Amalek from generation to generation. Thus, there is and will be an on-going warfare in which God enables His people to oppose every element that seeks to hinder them from going forward to enjoy His blessing.

Early Aggression against Enemies

Judah took the lead to fight the Canaanites. These were the original and dominant people of the land. They were characterized by a religious system that was evil and immoral. These people descended from Canaan, the son of Ham and dwelt in the lowlands toward the sea and in the valleys (Num. 13:29). They had evidently mingled with people from previous migrations into the area, including the Amorites and the Hurrians, both coming from the northeast. At times the Amorites are seen as a separate people (Num. 13:29; Josh. 11:3), but at other times, the name is used to include the Canaanites (Josh. 24:15, 18).

The Canaanites were prosperous merchants with strong armies (*"chariots of iron"* 4:3), and had much that naturally would be envied, thus "Canaanite" came to mean "trader, merchantman." They worshipped Baal, the sun god who also controlled the storms, the rain and affected the harvest. This worship was characterized by religious practices that were "terribly licentious" (Fausset) and evil. Ashtaroth was the female deity of this religion.

Dr. Wood suggests that if the worshippers of Baal had better crops than the Israelites, or if Israel's crops failed while the pagan worshippers of Baal had good crops, this would have been a strong inducement to forsake Jehovah. Since "Baal" means "lords, or masters," these people could have claimed to the Israelites that they, too, worshipped Jehovah, but only under a different name. We think of the experience of the psalmist in Psalm 73. He *"was envious at the foolish, when I saw the prosperity of the wicked"* (v. 3). His only solution was to flee to the presence of God that he might receive a clear understanding of their actual position and that his soul might be refreshed and strengthened by God. He had almost slipped and fallen, but he was strengthened in the Lord (vv. 23-26). This is what we need to preserve us from becoming *"like them that go down into the pit"* (Ps. 28:1).

Do we not encounter many today who are like Canaanites, claiming to worship God truly and yet with only a form of religion that seems right to them? We remember Paul's admonition to Timothy concerning those who are characterized by having *"a form of godliness but denying the power thereof"* (2 Tim. 3:5). The wise writer of Proverbs 16:25 warns us, *"There is a way that seemeth right unto a man, but the end thereof are the ways of death."* Those warnings hold true today and we dare not disregard them if we desire to continue in a faithful pathway for the Lord.

Canaanites seem to represent the tendency toward commercial activity with a view to becoming rich, which has ensnared many of the saints. Paul reminds Timothy, *"But they that will be rich fall into temptation and a snare, and into many foolish and hurtful lusts, which drown men in destruction and perdition"* (1 Tim. 6:9). In the next verse, we learn that it is the love of money (not money itself) that is a root of all evils. What has occurred in the past is still true today. Many a saint that had potential for God has been ruined in the very thing that God has entrusted to him to use as a stewardship in His service.

We learn that Ephesus was a very wealthy city, with three trade routes entering it, thus making it a commercial center for the area. In addition, the temple of Diana (Artemis), located in this city, made it a depository for much of the wealth of the world at that time. The saints of Ephesus, where the first opposition to the gospel came from prosperous artisans of the Diana craft (Acts 19:23-27), would have to overcome the love of money and the desire to be wealthy in order to maintain faithfulness to God and His Word.

It is not hard to see, even in our day, that when there is materialism and when the saints are well off financially, there is often a decline in their spirituality and exercise for the things of God. Material riches tend to stifle the desire for spiritual riches. Therefore, at the beginning, this was an enemy to be conquered by Judah.

Judah as the Leader

Judah took the lead by divine selection. Judah had been given the place of leadership from the beginning (Gen. 49:10) and had led through the wilderness journey (Num. 10:14). Now God gave them primary responsibility to lead the attack against the Canaanites. It is commendable that they invited Simeon to participate. Fellowship in the work of the Lord is always right and best, so we find these two tribes fighting side by side in this chapter (1:3, 17). However, though this demonstrates fellowship in the work, fighting enemies is more an individual matter, and this act of Judah seems to indicate a lack of confidence in God to give the victory. God had promised that they would be victorious (Judg. 1:2), so they needed no help from another tribe. In times when God expected them to fight and work together, it seems that they often failed to do so; however, in this case, God had not directed Simeon to go to the battle with Judah.

It is sad to note that in this case, the Lord directed Judah to go up first against the enemy to drive them out. At the end of the book, however, the Lord again directs Judah to go up first to battle, but this time it is against his brother, Benjamin (20:18). Simeon, the tribe to the south, accompanied Judah at the first, but in the end of the book, Judah led the way into battle against the tribe directly to their north. It seems that the pathway between the two references is, with its ups and downs, a pathway of degeneration and sad decline. Such is also the history of the professing church since the beginning, so that we look back on a course that has mirrored the experience of Israel.

This initial indication of weakness is amplified in chapter 1:19, where we read that Judah *"could not drive out the inhabitants of the valley, because they had chariots of iron."* That could hardly have been the case, since Barak and Deborah defeated a mighty force of Canaanites in Judges 4, and that host had 900 chariots of iron (ch. 4:3). The problem was not the force of the enemy; it was rather the inability of Judah to realize and depend on the power of God, now more severely seen than at the beginning. They had limited the Lord's power at the first, with the result that they lacked sufficient strength when they needed it most.

In the case of the assembly in Ephesus, we find that they had power to overcome the foe and to judge those who had false claims to be apostles (Rev. 2:2). They had maintained outward fidelity to the truth and had fought against evil. How commendable to see this at the beginning! It represents for us the contentions of the "church fathers" against early appearances of evil doctrines and practices that sought to infiltrate the church in those days. We owe much to their contending for the faith and thank God for their fidelity to the Word in these vital doctrines.

Adoni-bezek Recompensed

Victories resulted, because the Lord delivered the Canaanites into their hand (1:4). Adoni-bezek, one of the kings of the Canaanites, was captured and brought to Jerusalem. He suggests, by his past practices, the desire and power of the flesh to dominate and control others. His name seems to mean "lord of Bezek," or "lord of lightning," and it may suggest the dazzling effect of the devil's allurements that conquer men and bring them into subjection. He had humbled and maimed 70 kings so that they ate food like dogs under his table. Mephibosheth, responding to David's grace in 2 Samuel 9, expressed his gratitude by voluntarily being willing to eat from under David's table, but he sat at the table as one of the King's sons. This is our position in Christ, but this man, Adoni-bezek, represents an element that is far different. He, now under God's judgment, receives what he had sown (Gal. 6:9) and died in Jerusalem in that condition. Does this suggest that men, who act under the influence of the flesh to dominate and control others, will eventually receive in God's time the same results in themselves? This enemy constantly has to be overcome by each of us, for he unceasingly motivates desires to rise up to dominate others.

Victory at Hebron

Judah defeated the Canaanites who inhabited Hebron and possessed that ancient city of many memories for Israel. Signifying "communion," it would be a very important point in the experience of the saints. That fellowship, which is centered alone on the person of Christ and that forms the basis of our assembly gatherings is vital and must be possessed and enjoyed by all in fellowship in an assembly. There are elements that would oppose this important principle, either by undermining the terms of it (allow anyone to participate in assembly fellowship because they claim to be a Christian) or by minimizing the importance of it and acting contrary to it. We are exhorted by Paul in Ephesians 1:1-3 to "*endeavor* [give diligence] *to maintain the unity of the Spirit in the bond of peace.*" May we do all we can to foster and strengthen the cords of fellowship that bind us to the saints of God and may we enjoy fellowship with God!

Othniel Encouraged

It is a delightful picture that we see in Judges 1:11-15, where Othniel, motivated by love for Caleb's youngest daughter, went against Kirjath-sepher and possessed it, changing its name to Debir. We understand that Kirjath-sepher means "City of the book," but that name was changed to Debir, meaning "oracle," or "sanctuary." Both meanings of Debir indicate something more particular to the revelation of God's mind and person than just a book; it is a personal, direct expression of God manifesting His person and speaking to His saints through the power of His Word. The book becomes something with life and vitality, and surely this is what we need in our own lives that we might be sustained and guided in life and service.

Another lesson we learn from Othniel and Achsah is the importance, essential in every day, of believers seeking partners for life who are godly and spiritual. We are told nothing about her beauty externally, but it is evident that she was beautiful internally, spiritually, and that she was a great help to her husband in the things of God. Is it possibly due to her influence on him that he became the first judge of Israel who delivered them from the hand of the enemy (ch. 3:9-10)? It seems that young people (older as well?) have a tendency in some cases to enter into a marriage relationship without considering the impact that relationship will have on their spiritual life or their future usefulness for God. May this be an example to us in our decisions of this nature.

Then Achsah moved him to ask of her father a field, that is, possessions in the land linked with a man who was a constant overcomer, Caleb. The gift of the land caused a request for the springs of water, and she received both the upper and nether (lower) springs. The upper spring might suggest the work of the Spirit to bring divine refreshment and blessing, while the lower suggests the work of the Spirit to enhance our fellowship with other saints. Both are a blessing to our souls and serve to strengthen us in our pathway of faithful service for the Lord in His absence.

Applying this to the early days of the church, we observe that there was something evidently lacking, we understand, about the writings of those who followed the apostles in church history. That is, in those writings "we do not find the recognition of the presence and power of the Spirit." (C. A. Coates). We read in Andrew Miller's *Church History*, that these men "seem to have completely forgotten – judging from the Epistles which bear their names – the great New Testament truth of the Holy Spirit's presence in the assembly." This failure to realize the need for the work of the Holy Spirit would cause the failures seen in Israel and also in believers beginning early in this church age. If Judah had appreciated the power of God by His Spirit in them, they would have thought little of the chariots of iron and would have defeated the Canaanites nonetheless. If believers of any age fail to take into account the infinite power of God's Spirit at their disposal to use in this battle, they will not overcome the enemy and go on to possess their spiritual inheritance from God.

Increasing Power of Enemy

As the chapter progresses, we easily detect the increasing power and influence of these nations. Instead of driving them out and destroying them, Israel began to accommodate them, became accustomed to living among them, and accepted them. Note the change as the chapter proceeds: Judah destroyed 10,000 of the Canaanites and Perizzites (v. 4); Judah and Simeon "utterly destroyed" Zephath and then took Gaza, Askelon, and Ekron (only to lose them later) (vv. 17, 19); Judah *"could not drive out the inhabitants of the valley because they had chariots of iron"* (v. 21), *"Benjamin did not drive out the Jebusites… but they* **dwell among** *Israel unto this day"* and then Naphtali did not drive out the inhabitants of Bethshemesh nor Beth-anath, *"but he* **dwelt among** *the Canaanites"* (v. 33). Then in verse 34, the Amorites would not suffer the children of Dan to come down into the valley. So we see that the initial power of Israel over their enemies began to diminish and the power of the enemies seemed to increase.

This change was due solely to their lack of confidence in their God and their unwillingness to obey His Word. They ended up compromising with them, and these nations did exactly what God had told them they would do: they were thorns in their sides (2:3) and their gods were a snare to them. Instead of every generation learning war and how to fight (3:2), they learned, instead, how to compromise and get along. This change was insidious and occurred gradually, but its result was sure.

We compare this with the early activities of saints as recorded in 1 Corinthians and other epistles, and we find that this tendency has always been seen. When it prevails, there is weakness and conformity to the world that surrounds us. Today, we must acknowledge, that instead of believers being in the world but not of it, they are becoming more and more like the world. We are bringing the pleasures of the world and its entertainment into our homes. This will only break down the resistance of our children to its enticements and develop an appetite in them for worldly pleasures. Perhaps we do not realize what the future will be if this is the pattern of today. If we rear our children on a diet of worldly amusements, their appetite will only be whetted for more as they grow older, with the result that a subsequent generation will be even weaker spiritually than the present. May God preserve us and reinforce in our hearts the importance of raising our children in the *"nurture and admonition of the Lord"* (Eph. 6:4).

We note in chapter 1:18 that Judah had early victories over the Philistines, but those victories were incomplete. These people, representing religious men who occupy the land that rightfully belongs to God's people, were a constant threat and obstacle to the peace of Israel. Here, the victory was partial in that they failed to take Gath, and later in David's life, this city was the home of the giant Goliath. In addition, this enemy was the last enemy recorded in Judges and the period of Philistine bondage was the longest in the book. We also note that these cities were only occupied temporarily, since they were again in Philistine hands later in the book. It shows us the importance of getting complete victory over spiritual enemies that are so near and who have such a strong effect on our spiritual life. It is the thing that is near, *"sin that doth so easily beset us"* (Heb. 12:1), that causes us the greatest and longest-lasting problem.

Compromise at Bethel

Coming to chapter 1:22-26, we find that in seeking to take Bethel, formerly Luz ("departure, bent, perverseness"), the spies (sending spies was always an indication of lack of confidence in God, i.e., Deut. 1:21-22) encountered a man from the city. In return for his information that showed them the entrance, they let him go free. Bethel was a vital place in God's purposes, full of sacred memories of Jacob's experience with God in Genesis 28 and also later. This place, "house of God," had to be possessed and its character changed from a place of departure to a place signifying subjection to God's control where God's people would gather. In seeking a man's help, the spies allowed him to perpetuate the system that he represented, something God wanted destroyed. Again we see the early departure indicated by their action, displaying a lack of confidence in God to work and overcome the city without man's help.

Many, who have presently seemed to have escaped God's judgment, continue to perpetuate religious elements that are contrary to His will and purpose. The name, Luz, in relation to God's Word, seems to speak of those who pervert the truth and bend it to their own desires. There is no lack of men who are willing to use God's Word in this way; we must always seek to handle and use it reverently and honestly, *"rightly dividing"* it as to its proper interpretation and right application (2 Tim. 3:15). The truth of God's Word is always true and straight, and it would lead one to the house of God represented by a local assembly today. However, when believers seek the help of the world, an apparent victory may be obtained, but what has been done only allows the evil system to be continued in a different place.

We note, with thanksgiving, that the assembly in Ephesus had *"tried them which say they are apostles, and are not, and hast found them liars"* (Rev. 2:2). They recognized those who were trying to warp and twist the truth and, the Lord says, *"canst not bear them which are evil."* However, there were those, even in those early days of church history, who were compromising the truth and failing to allow it to have its full effect to guide God's people in their practices. Conditions are no different today, and we need to be careful in our handling of divine truth so that it will continue to preserve and direct God's people.

Angel of the Lord and God's Appeal

God mercifully moved to intervene and to recall them to Himself so that they might respond in self-judgment to be preserved (2:1-5). This angel of the Lord came from Gilgal, the place of circumcision in Joshua 14:6. Apparently, from the written record, they had not been to this place that signifies the cutting off of the flesh, i.e., judgment on that evil element that opposes God's work in our lives. His coming from Gilgal to Bochim to meet the people emphasizes that Gilgal is a place to which saints need to return constantly. The flesh always seems to grow of itself and repeatedly has to be dealt with in its various forms. Because they had not been to Gilgal spiritually, they were now in a place of weepers, which is what Bochim means.

The Angel reminded them of God's promise and God's work in the past through which God had brought them to the land. God had fulfilled His promises, but they had not obeyed His voice. Therefore, they would have to reap the results of their failure and experience the disciplining hand of God. This would result in them having to overcome or be overcome by their enemies.

Sadly, their only response to this searching message was two-fold: they wept and they offered sacrifices to the Lord. We do not know whether this was a burnt offering or a sin offering, but apart from that record, we are shocked to see that there was so little indication of any exercise to correct their actions. Maybe we should not be so shocked after all. Are there not times when God convicts us of failure in our lives, disobedience in our service, lack of responsiveness to Him, and lukewarmness on our part as in Laodicea? But while there may be weeping with determination to present our worship to God or to correct our lives, the effect doesn't seem to continue to bring about a lasting change for the better.

Left their First Love

What was the problem? It seems that it was the same in their day as the problem that afflicted the saints in Ephesus in Revelation 2:4: they had left their first love. Their hearts were not fervent and warm toward God, they were not as responsive to Him as they might have been in the past, and as a result, they were soon attracted to objects other than the Lord. Peter warns the saints in His day, *"But sanctify the Lord God in your hearts: and be ready always to give an answer to every man that asketh you a reason of the hope that is in you with meekness and fear: having a good conscience..."* (1 Pet. 3:16-17a). If Christ is not set apart, given the preeminent place in our **hearts**, then He will not have that place in our **lives**.

The Lord tenderly but severely challenges the saints of Ephesus to search their hearts. Peter was challenged by the Lord in

John 21, *"lovest thou me more than these?"* Jude warns us in his short epistle, *"keep yourselves in the love of God"* (v. 21). We note, by way of contrast, that John warns the saints, *"Little children, keep yourselves from idols"* (1 Jn. 5:21). It is always a healthy exercise on our part to search our hearts to determine the depth of our love for the Lord. If our hearts are not settled on the Lord and those things that pertain to Him, idols will always attract and take us away. The last words of God to Israel through Moses in Deuteronomy were intended to touch and effect the condition of their hearts, *"O that there were **such a heart** in them, that they would fear me, and keep all my commandments always, that it might be well with them, and with their children for ever!"* (Deut. 5:29). Like us, this they had failed to do. In Revelation 2 we learn that this was a problem that began at the very start of the church age and continued throughout, causing all the problems that ensued.

Keep Thy Heart...

The life will always reflect the condition of the heart. Solomon failed to follow his own advice in Proverbs 4:23, when he said, *"Keep thy heart with all diligence, for out of it are the issues of life."* Our actions flow from our heart condition, and if the heart is truly right with God, then our ways and walk will reflect it. Some tell us, "God knows my heart," when their life and behaviour is not according to God's Word. Surely He knows, but if the heart is in true fellowship with and in love with the Lord, the outward appearance and behaviour will follow the pattern of seeking to please the Lord and to honour His name. Sadly, we also know that in Israel's history (and in ours), *"the heart is deceitful above all things and desperately wicked, who can know it?"* (Jer. 17:9) and it is an important work to make sure of the condition of our hearts in relation to the Lord.

This appearance and appeal of the angel of the Lord corresponds with the Lord's appeal to Ephesus: *"Remember therefore from whence thou art fallen, and repent, and do the first works"* (Rev. 2:5). This threat of the lampstand's (candlestick's) loss was real and imminent. This is the case in Judges 2 as well; the remainder of the chapter summarizes the subsequent history of Israel in those days. The rising of a generation that knew not the

Lord nor the works that He had done for Israel followed that condition; serving Baalim and forsaking the Lord, with all that accompanied that action, was the result (vv. 10-13). Whenever God's people turn away from Him, lacking true, fervent love that motivates and controls the life, they will inevitably turn to something of the world or self.

Baal was an imitation of the true God, one who claimed the title of "my lord, or master" and thus pretended to be the true God. The plurality of the word (Baalim) indicates that there were many forms of this god that were found in different localities, according to the particular desires of the people. This could suggest that there are many objects of our lives that vie with the Lord to control and master us; it may be one thing for one person and another thing for another. Evil and error can take many forms, and they all must be resisted. Whatever they are, the result is loss of spiritual power and lack of victory over enemies, resulting eventually in the disciplinary hand of God.

Mercy of God in Discipline

The servitude to enemies that resulted from this departure was, in one sense, an expression of the love of God for His people and was another aspect of His mercy. It was because He loved them and wanted them to realize the results of their departure from Him by experience that He sold them into the hand of these nations. It was for their recovery that He allowed it, and it was beneficial when it caused them to turn to Him in repentance and to call upon Him for deliverance.

We would think that the conditions that God allowed in sequential periods of church history in Revelation 2-3 were for the purpose of correcting a previously existing condition. In other words, to correct their having left their first love in Ephesus, God allowed the extremity of persecution in Smyrna to restore His people to Him. They were delivered from that condition of heart by suffering, then they were delivered from suffering by the favour of the world that is seen in Pergamos, etc. God only brings discipline on His own true children; this is the teaching of Hebrews 12:3-13. He disciplines every son whom He receives and He does it out of love for them and through a desire to receive their complete affection. This should curb any inclination on our part to quickly assume that someone suffering affliction is not a child of God. It would also prevent us from thinking that such experiences are due to sin in every case. It may be, but it may not be as well.

We also learn from 1 Peter 1:6-7 and from Hebrews 12 that such discipline is sometimes developmental in order to enhance the features that God wants to augment in our lives. It may be preventative, so that we might be kept from departure in the future. It may also be punitive, in the form of punishment, as a father would chasten his child. Whatever the reason, the motive on God's part is His love for us and His desire to have His people in complete harmony with Himself out of love for Him. May He preserve us in this day, when *"the love of many shall wax cold"* (Matt. 24:12). Once again the exhortation of Proverbs 4:23 is applicable, *"Keep thy heart with all diligence, for out of it are the issues of life."*

It is remarkable that in chapter 2:19, we read that *"when the judge was dead, that they returned, and corrupted themselves **more** than their fathers,"* as if to say, the correction that God brought and the revival effected by the judge was short-lived and temporary. It seems that this is often the case; promises and vows made to God during times of duress and trial often turn out to be not much more than words and without any lasting effect in our lives. God intends that His hand upon us in allowing circumstances to touch us would have a lasting, life-long result in our lives to cause more subjection to Him. We can also see this as the case for the larger aspect of the professing church in this age; revivals and recoveries are usually temporary, with a lapse afterwards bringing a worse condition than existed before. It is as if the discipline had never been felt nor the voice of God been heard.

It is worth noting that as often as we read that *"the children of Israel did evil in the sight of the Lord"* (7 times), we also read that the Lord *"sold them,"* or *"delivered them,"* or *"strengthened"* the enemy against them. This emphasizes that the enemies around them could not touch or conquer them unless the Lord allowed them to do it. Even their ability to overcome Israel and to bring them into subjection was only possible as God permitted it. If they had been obedient to His Word and faithful to Him personally, no surrounding enemy could have brought them into bondage.

We live in an enemy land, and we also are surrounded by spiritual foes, desperately wanting to overcome and subdue the people of God. What is the key to our survival and victory over them? It is not in the force of arms, nor in the strength of the ballot box. Neither is it in our personal, innate ability or intelligence. It lies solely in our obedience to God's Word and in our fidelity to the person of Christ. When anything comes between us and the Lord to interrupt our communion, or when we relax our exercise spiritually and become occupied with other things, the result is inevitable and we will be overcome by them. Peter says, *"for of whom a man is overcome, of the same is he brought in bondage"* (2 Pet. 2:19). This is spoken relative to those who have forsaken the right way and have deliberately gone astray, but the principle applies in every case. Many believers have begun well in their Christian life, but have failed to end well because of their lack of consistent determination to seek only to do *"the will of God from the heart"* (Eph. 6:6).

Servitude to Mesopotamia

The first enemy that came to dominate the Israelites was Mesopotamia under Chushan-rishathaim. It seems that this enemy likely came from some area in upper Mesopotamia, possibly an enemy properly called Habiru that lived in the northern part. This would put them nearer to the land of Israel and more likely to seek to invade the area. Since Israel had served the groves (Asherim) and Baal, God sold them into servitude to what they represented. Mesopotamia was the location of Ur and Babylon. These false gods were derived from that old worship, Babylonianism, and represented it in this particular form. This was the country, or area, from which Abraham had been called out in separation to God. They had failed to maintain that separation, so now they were under its domination. They didn't go back to that country, and these Israelites had actually never been there; rather that country and power came in to dominate them.

There is a resemblance between Mesopotamia and Egypt. Both were like oases in a desert and owed their existence and attractiveness to rivers that flowed, these being expressions of God's mercies to people living under the oppressive effect of a burning sun. Both Egypt and Mesopotamia had descended from and were linked in Canaan, their forefather, and in the case of Mesopotamia, Nimrod ("the rebel"), stands out in its history. One could see *"the god of this world"* (2 Cor. 4:4), pictured by Chushan-rishathaim ("blackness of double wickedness"), who still wants to overcome the child of God and oppose God's purposes of grace in us. Nimrod was descended from Cush, who was a son of Canaan (Gen. 10:6), so he was descended from the one who was associated with God's curse through Noah (Gen. 9:25).

The number eight in Scripture is linked with a new beginning, one more than a complete cycle of seven, so these years of servitude would bring them to a new beginning. It is also a number linked with resurrection, in that it was on the first day of the week, a new start after the old had passed, that our Lord rose triumphantly from the dead. Our ground of receiving power to live for God is through being raised from the dead to walk in newness of life (Rom. 6:4, 11). It is good to see that they only took eight years to come to the point of crying out to God for deliverance in contrast to the longer periods of time we see in their servitude later in the book. This would teach us that the people, at this stage of their experience with God, were more sensitive to the fact that they were not enjoying the liberty as God's people, so they were quicker to cry out to God.

We can become accustomed to conditions that are not God's will for us at all, and thus we become insensitive to the fact that we are actually under bondage. That may be bondage to wrong teaching, or it might be under the control of wrong habits and practices. Whatever it might be, we need to *"awake out of sleep"* (Rom. 13:11) and be delivered from that condition to serve the Lord afresh. We see God's work to deliver as we move to the next chapter and look at Othniel, the first judge.

5

First Recovery Under Othniel
Smyrna and Persecution
Second Enemy: Moab

Characteristics of the Judges

There is a line of common characteristics that these judges possessed. Not all exhibited these marks to the same degree. There were some elements that all displayed, and one of those was a certain degree of valour, a willingness to face the foe in their dependence on God to work. Admittedly, Barak seems to be an exception to this, but he did fight the enemy when encouraged and strengthened by Deborah. We notice that, in many cases, they were willing to engage the enemy without any promise of support from their own nation, such as in the case of Ehud and Samson. This shows us that one who would lead and deliver God's people must be willing to step out in faith in God, depending on Him to work despite the obstacles. Gideon is the most remarkable of these, in that after God depleted his ranks so that only 300 remained, he went to fight an innumerable host of the Midianites and won a victory. Samson is different, but he also engaged the Philistines without any support (only opposition) from Judah.

We also notice that these men usually displayed a great deal of concern and perception about the condition of their people. They were moved by the sense of dishonour that was being done to the Lord's name (e.g., Othniel, Ehud, and Gideon). They recognized the results that the enemies' oppression had with regard to the Lord's name among the nations and His people. Othniel's history is not fully developed, but we read that *"the Spirit of the Lord came upon him"* (Judg. 3:10), and he was moved to deliver the people. Ehud could say to Eglon, king of Moab, *"I have a message from God unto thee"* (Judg. 3:20), and then he was used of the Lord to bring deliverance to God's people. We think of Gideon threshing wheat in the winepress, and his response to the angel of the Lord was, *"Oh my Lord, if the Lord be with us, why then is all this befallen us?"* (Judg. 6:13). So we mark that there was a sense of outrage and concern for the prevailing conditions and how they touched the nature and character of the Lord and His promises.

In most of the cases, the judges displayed qualities of leadership, so that they were able to rally the people to follow them to war against the enemies. They seemed to be able to instill confidence into their followers so that they led the people into a battle against insurmountable odds but without any dissension or lack of desire expressed by their warriors. This quality seemed to be the result of several factors, one being that God had raised them up for this purpose. The response of the people was God's work in them that corresponded with His work in the leader. God's people seem instinctively to recognize the one who God has provided and who can give positive leadership in times of crisis.

In summary, the judges were usually marked by their capability, their commitment and their courage as they rose to God's call and effected a deliverance in their own day. Those qualities should mark anyone who would take such a position of leadership among the saints in any day. Those who are called of God to that place will also recognize that God has raised them up, and the Lord's people, if they have any spiritual perception, will respond by following them.

Othniel: The First Judge

To save them from the result of their sin, God raised a judge (a deliverer or saviour) named Othniel. His name means "powerful man of God," or "lion of God" and he showed it by his strength of character and willingness to stand up to the foe. Another possible meaning of his name is "seasonable speaking of God" and if this is its meaning, it would suggest God delivering His people by a word that moves His people and works powerfully to defeat the enemy. While we do not have apostles or even "Timothys," we do have what the Holy Spirit has given us, and that is the Word of God. It is a known and applied word that can be used in the actual situation like the Sword of the Spirit, which works effectually to deliver and bring restoration (Eph. 6:17; Heb. 4:12).

The deliverance for Israel was accomplished by the power of the Spirit of the Lord coming upon Othniel, so that it was a deliverance by God's hand rather than what men could accomplish in themselves. It is remarkable and important to note that this is the first instance in Holy Scripture of the Spirit of God coming on a man. As we note the circumstances and consider the exercise that must have accompanied his action, it shows us the availability of the Holy Spirit to provide the strength and resources needed for victory.

God Uses Small and Weak Elements

It is wonderful to see how God can use small things, almost insignificant things, to work out His purpose. In this book of Judges, we see seven small, weak, or insignificant things that God used: a left handed man (3:21), an ox goad (3:31), women (4:4, 18), a tent peg (4:21), a pitcher and trumpet (7:20), a millstone (9:53), and an ass's jawbone (15:16). So we learn that the essential factor in God's work is not ability; it is spirituality and the willingness to act under the authority of God through obedience to His Word.

Othniel's Characteristics

Othniel was a man who was linked with Hebron (Josh. 14:13-14) through Caleb, his father-in-law. It seems to be true, and is widely accepted by scholars, that he was likely also Caleb's younger brother, though this is not certain. The relationship between the two suggests typically that the source of his power lay in his abiding in communion with God. We note in John 15, that the criterion for fruitfulness and power lies in abiding in close communion with the Lord. Most assuredly a believer who is living in this condition can be used of God to deliver others who are not. Abraham was such a man in Genesis 14, where he came from Hebron (13:18) to deliver his carnal nephew Lot. We need such men today, those who are living near the presence of God and walking in submission to His will.

Othniel was not a novice when he was called to this work. He had already overcome the Anakim and possessed their city out of love for Achsah (1:12-15). God usually develops a leader by different acts of obedience prior to his being thrust into a larger sphere of service. In addition, considering the age of Caleb and the facts of the wandering in the wilderness, Othniel would not have been a young man. Dr. Leon Woods suggests that he might have been about seventy-five years old. He was a man of maturity who had developed and had proven himself in his life and service already.

Simply considered, Othniel represents a believer who has the ability to overcome obstacles in his Christian experience through the right condition of his heart in love with Christ. This quality would characterize one who was enjoying communion with his God. Everything about Othniel suggests those marks of spiritual quality that one would display who God can use to deliver His people. He was linked with a pure wife who had spiritual exercise, and she was not one from the nations around. He had taken the city of the book (representing man's wisdom) and made it an oracle of God, or God speaking through His Word. There is a vast difference between seeing God's Word as a book, putting it on equality or comparing it with other great books of men, and looking to it for God to speak to me personally. Those that God would use have come to value and long for God to speak to them through His own Word, and they have received it as it is in truth, *"the Word of God"* (1 Thess. 2:13). How precious it is to see this in any man or woman among God's people!

This relates to what was needed in the early days of the church (and is also needed today). In days of contention against heresies, Gnostic and otherwise, God raised men who used the Word of God to combat those false teachings and to establish the truth of vital doctrines that we hold today. Those were men who defended the deity of Jesus Christ, His eternal sonship, the truth of the gospel and the expanse of doctrines relating to salvation, as well as many other vital truths essential to the continuation of Christian testimony.

In addition, the proper use of God's Word always delivers saints of any day from the bondage and snare of the elements of the former life, the old world from which we have been saved. This is accomplished through its proper application by the power of the Spirit to change those conditions that were detrimental to the saint of God.

When we think of the significance of Othniel, we can link him with the encouragement of Christ to His people during the period of persecution represented by Smyrna. He only wrote a short word to this church, but it contained many reminders of God's faithfulness to strengthen them in the midst of trials and persecutions. It was during this time of church history that the Word's power and reality ministered strength to those who were experiencing the pressures placed upon them. It is what we need in our day as well, a seasonable word from God that lifts the heart and redirects our thoughts to place full confidence in the certainty of God's Power, as well as God's Word and its effectiveness in our lives.

We thank God for men in the past like Othniel, but we are also thankful for men of this character in the present. We constantly need believers who move and live in the same character as Othniel, whether in what we observed in chapter 1:13-15 where he and his wife sought blessing to produce fruitfulness in their land, or here in his conquest of the great enemy of God's people.

Vacuum in Leadership

Othniel's further history is scanty. God only records that he judged Israel and that a period of peace and rest existed for forty years. The "rest" under his judgeship indicates that the victory over Mesopotamia was complete and they were free of oppressing foes for a prolonged period. It seems that later victories might not have been so complete since, in those cases, the mention of rest is omitted. Early victories seem to have been more complete.

The forty years of rest seem to be typical. Forty is a number in Scripture that indicates man's complete testing according to his responsibility before God (4 x 10). Surely God was testing Israel to see if, in such conditions, they would continue to remain faithful to Him, even after the passing of a great leader. Is it not often true, and we see it so many times in this book, that under the influence of a strong individual who leads the people of God by his godly influence and ability to use God's Word, the saints are preserved and go on for the Lord? It is often true that upon his death, those same ones quickly depart out of the way and degenerate into practices that are contrary to his teaching. This has been seen repeatedly in local assemblies, and the results are always very sad to observe. If the eye of the people does not look beyond the man who leads them, when he is gone, they will forget that ultimately God must guide and rule His people.

It was near the end of Moses' first forty days on the mount with God that the people insisted that Aaron build a false god (Ex. 32:1-2). Since they had their eyes on a man, a human deliverer and leader, they had forgotten that God was still in the camp with them and expected their obedience. Moses' absence revealed the true condition of their hearts, and they failed to be faithful to the Lord, though they had solemnly promised to do so not many days previously (Ex. 19:8; 24:3, 7). The passing of a leader who has positively affected God's people will test their fidelity to the Lord and reveal how deep their exercise is to obey His Word.

Departure Again!

Just a simple statement, yet how full of meaning! They did evil **again** in the sight of the Lord. This oft-repeated revelation of their condition indicates that in every one of us there is an evil heart of unbelief that tends toward departure from the living God (Heb. 3:12). It behooves us to be on guard constantly, not only against that which is without, but with concern for what lurks within.

Another Enemy Rises

Notice that it was the Lord who strengthened Eglon (3:12). This indicates that his ability to move against Israel was due to

God's hand allowing and enabling him. By his characteristics and link with Moab, we learn that this king typifies the power of the flesh to overcome the saints. It is a form of the flesh that is gross and corrupt. It is self-indulgence expressed in desires and practices. The fact that he was *"a very fat man"* with an army of fat men (Judg. 3:17, 29) speaks of the natural tendency of the flesh to indulge itself and to grow out of proportion as a result. It is a "condition of things easily nourished" and needs to be combated in every one of us. None are without a natural tendency to indulge the flesh and to feed the "ego."

In this enemy, we see pictured to us the natural tendency of each one of us to allow the flesh and its evil inclinations to dominate a child of God. It is evident that whenever this is allowed, the flesh eventually becomes the master. Peter taught this in his second epistle: *"While they promise them liberty, they themselves are the servants of corruption: for of whom a man is overcome, of the same is he brought in bondage"* (2 Pet. 2:19). We see also that Eglon was one who indulged his comforts, sitting in his summer parlor, pampering himself and enjoying his life (Judg. 3:20). How natural this is in all of us; it is a great hindrance to the saints possessing and enjoying their spiritual blessings!

One has said that Moab also stands for mere profession of Christianity (F. W. Grant, *Numerical Bible*), living on the border of the land without actually entering in. The rise of men with false professions of Christianity was evident in the period of church history that followed the period of persecution, so that, under Constantine's rule, many adhered outwardly to Christianity. As a result of this departure, many problems came in to oppress and distress God's people.

Nearby Enemy

Israel had overcome Moab in battle when they entered the land (Num. 22:1; Josh. 24:9). That victory occurred about 80 years prior to these events. New men had risen in Moab as well as in Israel, and this shows that the need to fight enemies never ceases. Our spiritual foes never cease, and while there may be a short respite from the warfare, we can be sure that they will not rest from their efforts to overcome the saints.

In contrast to their first enemy, Mesopotamia, which was a distant land, Moab was one that was very near to Israel. We think of Moab as a country that represents those who have a Christian profession, but with the flesh still in control. This is something that seems very near at hand regarding church testimony in any day, and particularly in the period represented by Pergamos. It is one thing to combat enemies that lie at a distance and are somewhat removed from the saints, but it is another thing and more difficult to resist what seems so near that it is almost a part of us. In this we see the stronger influence of the tendencies of the flesh, since it is an evil element that lies within, truly a part of us by nature. As such, we are more willing to tolerate it rather than deal with it in judgment as is necessary (Gal. 5:24). The believer must be careful not to accommodate evil practices that seem so innocuous and harmless! They may be just the things that will bring about his downfall.

Trinity of Evil

In addition, here we see a trinity of evil in the enemy; Eglon of Moab was linked with Ammon, which typifies the violence of the flesh in its acts toward others, and with Amalek, typifying the destructive and profane aspect of the flesh. Both Moab and Ammon descended from Lot through his daughters, a very evil beginning that continued through the course of their history, while Amalek came from Esau. All three of these continued to be inveterate enemies of God's people, and the same is always true in the spiritual realm.

Extent of Domination

We notice that this enemy invaded the land and possessed the *"city of palm trees,"* which clearly was Jericho. Jericho was the location of their earliest victory as they began to possess the land (Josh. 6) and this enemy was acting effectively to erase the triumphs of their history. Is this possible with us? We think of saints who once gained the victory over the flesh and who saw God's power manifested to enable them to vanquish evil habits of the past and to subdue all that was contrary to God in their lives. What about now? Is it possible that the enemy called "self" and "self-indulgence" has come in to retake the old ground with all its former pleasantness? When we think of the years Israel continued under this domination, we can clearly see a picture of the reality of some believers' lives; if once retaken by old sins and fleshly activity, they often continue for many years under its control without crying to God for deliverance.

For Eglon and Moab to find assistance in Ammon and Amalek indicates that Moab was dominating the nations of that area. There was not enough area for all those nations to exercise sovereignty, so that when one rose to prominence, the others were subjugated. We also note that for Eglon to cross the Jordan to the west bank and establish a headquarters in Jericho indicates that Reuben, at the least, had suffered loss of territory and liberty since Moab was from the area of that tribe. Also of interest is the fact that Jericho had lain in ruins since its defeat under Joshua. Archeologically, the majority of the ruins had been left untouched; except for one area, including a building on top of a hill above a spring, that had been rebuilt dating back to the time of Eglon (*Distressing Days of the Judges*, Leon Wood).

Significance of Gilgal

It is noteworthy that the extent of his domination was only to Gilgal (3:19). If Jericho was the place of a great former victory, Gilgal was the place of judgment on the flesh pictured by the circumcision of the flesh (Josh. 5:2-9). As F. W. Grant has put it, "The memorials of death passed through and a resurrection standing will necessarily be outside of Moab's possession." The empty professor can see no value in a link with Christ in glory and a position that is outside the environs of the world's influence.

The fact that this was as far as he seems to have gone indicates that there is some measure of residual power in the believer's life that stems from that judgment on the flesh that was a part of his salvation. Gilgal also was where they had fed on the food of Canaan for the first time, the *"old corn of the land"* (Josh. 5:11) and that feeding seemed to restrain his ability to control. Feeding on this food would teach us the need to feed on Christ Himself, who is the firstfruits from the dead and is now the risen Man in the glory. Colossians 3:1-4 tells us of this importance: *"If ye then be risen with Christ, seek those things which are above, where Christ sitteth on the right hand of God. Set your affection on things above, not on things on the earth."*

We know that it is our occupation with Christ in the glory, triumphant over sin, hell and death that will preserve the child of God from fleshly domination. It seems that this attraction and truth had failed to speak to those who occupied the period that Pergamos represents. They were indulging themselves and enjoying the favour and acceptance of the world. No longer were they unpopular and persecuted; now they were accepted and others were being pressed into professions for Christ. As a result, the flesh and its desires for expression found more latitude and acceptance.

Expression of Domination

This enemy dominated and demanded tribute of the people for 18 years, resulting in their finally crying to the Lord for deliverance. That demanded tribute was an expression of their acknowledged servitude to Moab. It must have been a humiliating experience for them to pay yearly tribute to a dominating oppressor. Each year would remind them that they were not free, that this enemy controlled them.

Could that be true in some saints? Year after long year, they continue in realized bondage to habits from which they once were free but now have been overtaken by them again. Is it possible that there is no desire for deliverance? If there is, then there is power to liberate the child of God, for *"greater is He that is in you than he that is in the world"* (1 Jn. 4:4). How interesting that while Chushan-rishathaim dominated the people for only 8 years, in this case, 18 years pass without deliverance or expressions of any concern for liberation. Is it possible that saints are more ready to tolerate this form of evil rising from the flesh within than they are willing to accommodate that which results from the former life? However it may be, the time came when they did cry and we find that the Lord responded to that cry to raise up a deliverer to the people. It is evident that this is always the case. Hezekiah said, *"the Lord was ready to save me"* (Isa. 38:20) and we have often found that to be true.

6

Second Recovery Under Ehud
Pergamos and Compromise
Third Enemy: Canaan

Ehud: A Defective Judge

For their deliverance, in His mercy, God raised a very un-
likely man! Ehud means "confession" (F. W. Grant), or "united"
(Brown, Driver, Briggs) and he was a son of Gera, a word meaning "pilgrimage" or "combat" (Jackson). There also seems to be
the element of praise involved in his name.

If these suggestions are true, Ehud represents a man who
stands out from mere profession. His clear confession as a spiritual pilgrim was marked by a life that demonstrated reality,
something that should characterize every believer. It is also the
character that a leader among the saints, one who would be exercised to deliver God's people, **must** display. The result is that
from the united character he displayed, God received praise and
honour and God's people were restored. Gera was a son of Benjamin, the smallest tribe of Israel, but a tribe out of which came
many mighty men. The last son of another Gera mentioned in
our Bible is found in 2 Samuel 16:5—Shimei. Instead of blessing
God's people, we know him for his act of cursing David, God's
king. This son of Gera, Ehud, was a man used of God to bless.

Benjamin, whose name means "son of my right hand," was
the last son of Jacob. Rachel wanted to call him "Ben-ammi,"
signifying "son of my sorrow," but Jacob overruled in the name.
The two names speak of the two-fold character of Christ; Ben-
ammi pertains to His suffering and sorrow while Benjamin
speaks of His exaltation and glory. Ehud, being of Benjamin,

would speak to us of a man who is linked spiritually and is in fellowship with the triumphant and glorified Man at God's right hand, our Lord Jesus Christ. Such a man can move in power to accomplish a victory for God and His people, and it is the position that we all should know personally in our lives for God. Only such leaders can overcome the flesh and deliver themselves and God's people.

Eglon and Moab

In addition, Eglon and Moab were primarily intruding upon the territory of Benjamin (and Ephraim, apparently), so this enemy was depriving them of the inheritance that God had given them. Is not this the case, whether in the period of Smyrna, Pergamos or presently? In the case of Smyrna, the enemy was seeking to vanquish the testimony of Christ by force; in Pergamos, the world sought accommodation and compromise so that the church became united with the world. When the flesh and self gain power in the lives of believers, there is always a loss of spiritual territory that God wants them to enjoy.

We think of scriptural principles and practices that were given us in contrast to compromise with the world during that time of favour pictured by Pergamos. We relate that era represented in the letter to the assembly in Pergamos (Rev. 2:12-17), to the period of church history during which there was world favour. Constantine professed conversion to Christianity, and the result was that instead of being persecuted, to be a believer was popular.

However, the simplicity of assemblies gathered under the leadership of local elders gave way to a hierarchy of pastors, bishops, archbishops and ultimately, popes that God's Word never taught. The requirement for reality of life to prove the genuineness of profession was succeeded by reception into churches of those who simply agreed with accepted doctrines. The necessity of genuine conversion to God as a work of the Holy Spirit was supplanted by using the rite of baptism to make converts. The list could go on, but to summarize, unscriptural practices were introduced that catered to the flesh, which resulted in sad effects in the church sphere that are yet seen in their domination today.

On an individual level, how many saints who once continued well for God have lost the priceless spiritual possessions that they once claimed and enjoyed? Whenever the flesh and self are allowed an entrance and are not judged, the result will be loss in truth, principles, and practices among us. Ehud clearly speaks to us of an exercised man who is aware of how much has been lost personally and collectively, and in his concern for this and the honour of God, is willing to be used to deliver them.

It is notable that Ehud, while raised up of the Lord to deliver Israel, is not said to have had the Spirit of God come on him for that work. It seems to indicate a lower level of spirituality in him than Othniel demonstrated (3:10). Yet, even with that consideration, he was a man who encouraged the Lord's people (3:28) and who God used to deliver them. It shows us that God can use those who have an exercise and are yielded to His hand, even if they may not have the same degree of spiritual power as others might possess.

Ehud's Limitation

In addition, God calls attention to the fact that he was left-handed. The men of Benjamin seem to be characterized by being left-handed (Judg. 20:16; 1 Chron. 12:2). In the case of Ehud, however, this may be more than a family, inherited trait. In this case, the expression means, "one defective in the right hand, or shut of the right hand." If so, it indicates that he was not one who could depend on his own power of self. In this sense, we learn that God can raise and use those who do not have the ability that others might possess, since it is not ability nor inability that matters in the things of God. He can give ability and is able to use whomsoever He will. To be fair, though, some writers say that this means that he had the unique ability to use both hands equally (Barnes, Clarke, and Jamieson, Fausset and Brown, etc.). However, Keil and Delitzsch say that it indicates one who could not use his right arm effectively. Whatever it may be, he was one who was available for God's use and was evidently exercised for this work, since he had prepared a dagger, or short sword, to bring about the deliverance of God's people.

Ehud's Preparation

Ehud was the man in charge of the delegation that brought the yearly tribute to Eglon in Jericho. He may have been a man of some standing in Israel; such a man would sense his own responsibility to seek to deliver his own people. Surely there are those in a similar position among saints today who would willingly give all they have to restore the saints and deliver them from adverse conditions. We need them in every day! Knowing this ahead of time, he evidently began to prepare in view of using the occasion to defeat this evil foe.

This only reinforces the truth that preparation in secret, alone with God, and in anticipation of the opportunity to be used, is essential for any service. There are many among the saints who have greater ability in every area of life, including possession of gifts given by God and including natural abilities that could be directed toward His service. However, through lack of discipline, lack of exercise or through lack of desire, they waste their time and lives in activities that result in their being useless for God's work. One simply cannot stand in public and effectively minister to the saints to help and deliver them if he has not spent time in secret with God, whetting the Sword of the Word and learning how to use it effectively. It is serious business to be used by God to bring deliverance and blessing, and this cannot come through the work of those who are occupied with material gain or personal pleasure. Those who are most used of God have paid a price to do so through learning the truths of God's Word by diligent application to its study and by developing the ability to use it properly. This is the advice of Paul to Timothy (2 Tim. 2:15) that was essential in his day of departure.

His main preparation consisted of making the short, sharp two-edged sword that he used to deal with Eglon. No doubt, he had devised the purpose that he would take advantage of when he was involved in delivering the tribute money to Eglon. He not only had the **plan**, but he had made the **preparation** in view of action. This sharp, two-edged sword is certainly symbolic of the Word of God. The Lord, writing to the church in Pergamos, said that He was the one who had the sword with two edges (Rev. 2:12). There were conditions that He discerned and revealed to them that required the use of the Word of God applied in its power. It is not, at this point, its work to comfort and assuage the troubled. It is its work to reveal, convict, correct and instruct in the truth of God (2 Tim. 3:16-17). A sword with two edges would cut both ways. Some may be able to use the sword mightily to expose and correct the faults of others, but they may be reluctant to use that same sword on themselves. Any leader who would be effective in delivering saints must be one whose life is exposed and transparent to the Word of God and who is constantly being assessed by its ability to judge the individual believer, including himself. To apply divine truth to others without having applied it in its force to ourselves is to tread in unfelt territory to our own ruin rather than the blessing of the saints.

Ehud bound the sword on his right thigh under his clothing (Judg. 3:16). It was there so it would be ready to use with his left hand, and in that position it was also not being displayed outwardly so as to call the attention of Eglon. Think of the words of Hebrews 4:12 in this regard: *"For the word of God is quick, and powerful, and sharper than any two-edged sword, piercing even to the dividing asunder of soul and spirit, and of the joints and marrow, and is a discerner of the thoughts and intents of the heart."* We think also of 1 Peter 3:15, *"But sanctify the Lord God in your hearts: and be ready always to give an answer to every man that asketh you a reason of the hope that is in you with meekness and fear."* We need those today, as in every day, who can use the Word of God effectively to accomplish whatever work is for the honour of God and the blessing of His people. It isn't through public display of the Word as if to flaunt its qualities and professed power; it is through its intelligent use that the enemy is overcome and the saints delivered.

Ehud's Performance

After leading the delegation of those who bore the tribute gift (*minchah*, the word signifying a gift from an inferior to a superior...the same word as "meat offering" or "meal, gift offering" in Lev. 2) to Eglon, Ehud sent them away. It seems that he accompanied them as far as the quarries at Gilgal, then turned back. "Quarries" means "graven" and is usually used for graven images (Deut. 7:5, 25). Unless there had been very serious departure so that graven images were set up in this most sacred place (possible, in view of the conditions), it seems to speak of the stones that were brought up out of Jordan and placed at Gilgal when Israel crossed over (Josh. 4:8, 21-24). They commemorated God's power to bring them into the land of His promise by annulling the power of death, pictured by Jordan. Their passing through the Red Sea pictures the believer's death to the old man and the world; it is emphasized that Israel went into the Red Sea (Ex. 14:22) but not that they came out.

In Jordan, the emphasis is on the fact that they came out, or *"passed over,"* rather than that they went in (Josh. 3:6, 11, 14, 16-17). Jordan seems to suggest the resurrection of the believer with Christ to walk in newness of life. These events together embrace the great truths that are expressed in baptism. We died with Christ and were raised to walk in newness of life in fellowship with our risen Lord. In Joshua's words to Israel, they were to remind their children that the stones were the evidence of the power of God so that they might fear the Lord their God all the days (Josh. 4:21-24). Had they not failed to appreciate the delivering power of their God and His great purpose for bringing them over and into the land?

F. C. Jennings says that

> "'Quarries' should be 'boundaries;' they are the boundary stones dividing between different estates or countries … it is the boundary between faith and unbelief; between the church and the world. It is the 'cross of the Lord Jesus Christ,' by whom the world is crucified to me and I to the world (Gal. 6:14)."

Ehud, returning to his conflict with Eglon after contemplating the stones at Gilgal, would have been reinforced in his confidence in God and the assurance that he was linked with the God of all power. This is what is always needed when there is any work to be done for God, especially when dealing with such a formidable enemy as the flesh! This truth would be reinforced even more by the mention of "Gilgal." This word means "rolling" and it was the location where the men of Israel were circumcised the second time (Josh. 5:2). The conflict ahead for Ehud was based on the principle expressed at Gilgal, which was the need for judgment on the flesh, cutting it off and removing it under condemnation of God. It was an exercise of separation from the binding power of a world system that is completely contrary to God and His Word.

Ehud's Conflict

Ehud returned with a secret errand (word, message) for Eglon. It was a message from God. It teaches us that it requires more than our own word to overcome this enemy; it is essential to apply the power of God's Word to the flesh and all that pertains to it. This is also a private work. There is work to be done in public, but there is also the need for a work to be done privately. This applies to each one of us individually, but it also speaks of the work of an overseer who is spiritual, as he seeks to restore an erring one in the spirit of meekness (Gal. 6:1). Only one who has applied the Word to himself can effectively use it to deal with others to restore them as well.

Eglon in his summer parlor ("upper room of coolness"), expresses the desire of the flesh for ease and self-indulgence. The prominence of those who sought positions of authority over others (and still do), setting aside the principles of church truth taught in God's Word, is an expression of fleshly ambition and desire for self-indulgence. Pergamos was a time during which the flesh within had more opportunity than ever to express and indulge itself. Pleasure was now available instead of persecution. Suffering was a thing of the past; now it was satisfaction in worldly activities. We have the same danger today, don't we?

Ehud recognized that there was no use negotiating with the flesh. Promises avail nothing, compromise is deadly, and nothing will do but to put the sword of God's Word to it to destroy its power. This is exactly what he did, using the sword that he had prepared to kill this terrible enemy of the saints. What he was doing was not primarily for self; it was on behalf of the Lord's people. When he plunged that sword into Eglon's belly (symbol of the center of his indulgence), it also revealed what was within this king. The awful contents that were covered by respectability were exposed. This shows us that the Word of God is living and powerful, truly able to expose what is within and to judge it according to God so as to bring deliverance (Heb. 4:12-13).

Ehud's Leadership

After returning again to Gilgal, having destroyed the enemy that held them, he called all Israel to the battle that would result from his personal exploit. Those Moabites who they took at the fords of Jordan were all men like their leader—fat men (Judg. 3:29). Is not it remarkable that there seems to be no lack of strength on the side of the flesh in its combat with the saints? But the believer, acting in the power of God and the Word of God, is able to defeat such an enemy and to overcome him for the deliverance of the saints.

Is not this what we particularly need in our day? Just as in past days, there is a need for leaders to act personally to judge the flesh and to lead the saints by spiritual power, so that the intruding and controlling principles that are connected with the flesh will be overcome and the saints delivered.

We do notice, however, that it only says that *"Moab was subdued that day under the hand of Israel"* (3:30). In contrast to other enemies, this one was not destroyed or completely overcome. It tells us that the enemy represented by Moab is a constant foe to the individual believer as well as to assembly testimony, and it repeatedly raises its ugly head to cause divisions, strife and great problems that have resulted in ruin to church testimony. The desire for place, the fighting for prominence and the constant efforts to assert oneself never cease, and this tendency must be combated constantly by the same weapon, the proper use of the Word of God.

Prolonged Peace under Ehud

It was of God's mercy that the land had rest for 80 years under the leadership of Ehud. Though a weak judge in many ways, he seemed to be marked by dependence on God that enabled him to preserve peace among Israel for a longer period of time than any other. Perhaps we do not need "strong" men in our assemblies, for they tend to assert themselves in their own strength. They have a tendency to think that they have great abilities that others should recognize and through which they are able to accomplish great things. The weak man is truly the strongest in God's economy, for he knows that he must depend on God and keep close through his constant communion with the Lord to fulfill the work.

Paul stated the principle in 2 Corinthians 12:9, saying, *"And he said unto me, my grace is sufficient for thee: for my strength is made perfect in weakness."* Such a man has greater power and effectiveness in God's things than any man who has wonderful personal ability in the natural realm. Would that God raised up many such men in our midst, men who are truly spiritual, controlled by the Spirit of God and led by the Word of God, so that we might have such peace for an extended period as well!

Further Foes to Combat!

However, the believer's foes have never ceased to exist. If we believe that there are no more enemies to overcome, we only deceive ourselves, and we will surely fail in our pathway of Christian life.

Shamgar's Victory

During this time we read about Shamgar, who used an ox goad (a very unusual weapon, but typical of Judges) to deliver Israel (3:31). Only one verse is devoted to his history, but we gather that he worked in the western area of Israel to combat the rising force of the Philistines while Ehud was more to the east. *"After this,"* seems to indicate that his victories occurred after Ehud's, but it is best to place him within the 80 years of rest. An ox goad, in the hands of a strong and capable man, would be able to wreak great damage on a foe. We learn that it was often 8 feet in length and as much as 6 inches in diameter at its large end, with the other end sharpened to a point. One can imagine the potential for such an instrument! Shamgar was evidently a man who, from his daily life and work, knew how to use an ox goad.

This teaches us that it is a believer's instrument, developed by daily use, which is skillful to destroy God's enemies. It reminds us of Hebrews 5:14, *"But strong meat belongeth to them that are of full age, even those who by reason of use have their senses exercised to discern both good and evil."* What Shamgar used in this case was a tool that he had exercised in his daily life, and this suggests that we need to develop our use of God's Word by daily study and application if we desire to be effective in the spiritual warfare. Then the Philistines would not suspect an ox goad when an Israelite farmer was carrying it! This instrument of death appeared to be common place to them, not worth their consideration, but in the hands of Shamgar, it had great power for deliverance. God's Word means little to the unsaved, yet it is the *"sword of the Spirit"* (Eph. 6:17). F. C. Jennings says,

> "The oxgoad in itself would be a fitting emblem of the Word of God. If, as Ecclesiastes tells us, *'the words of the wise are as goads,'* that is: sharp, pointed, effective to stir up, and to send along the pilgrim way any who would linger here, then the words of divine perfect wisdom must have peculiarly that character. I see therefore in this 'oxgoad' only another figure of the divine Word."

The text does not say whether he killed 600 Philistines at one time or over a longer period; either way, it was a great work of deliverance. Whether or not God had actually called him to be a judge (he is never spoken of as a judge), he was an exercised man who was not willing to allow the Philistines to make inroads into God's people's territory. What he did was important enough for the divine record to include his exploit for us to emulate. He was evidently a minor judge who was of sufficient importance for God to include him in the divine record. He did more than the other "minor" judges, in that he is the only one who brought about deliverance for Israel. God records the work and achievements of those who may not be so important as compared with others.

Regarding the tendency toward departure in Israel, we learn in chapter 4:1 that Israel was still the same; they had not changed after 80 years of rest. We are no different; what was written of them, that they *"did evil in the sight of the Lord,"* expresses the same natural tendency in any of us also. Even with constant vigilance, we often are not aware that the greatest enemy lies within! Carelessness, thinking that we stand (1 Cor. 10:12), will only decrease our care and expressed dependence on God for protection and deliverance.

The Next Enemy: Canaan

A period of relative peace prevailed for 80 years following Ehud's victory over Moab. Some extra-biblical sources give an indication why this was possible, apart from Israel possibly continuing in a measure of faithfulness to God during that time. One element, no doubt used of God to hold their enemies at bay, was that Egypt was actively moving in the southern part of Canaan and was exercising strong control in the region. This effect would have hindered Israel's neighboring nations from moving offensively against God's people (*Distressing Days of the Judges*, Leon Wood). God can and does use contentions between nations to hinder their activities of oppression toward His people when need be. However, that Egyptian influence apparently waned, and it gave opportunity for Jabin and Sisera to increase Canaanite domination and oppression of Israel. This was evidently coupled with Israel's increasing departure from the Lord that resulted in God bringing discipline on His people once again.

Judges 4 records the next enemy that Israel had to combat and overcome. Canaan, under the leadership of Jabin, was God's instrument in judging His people when they did evil in His sight.

In passing, one might note that it was during this particular time that the events of the book of Ruth occurred. This shows us that not all Israel departed from the Lord and sunk into idolatry. While Ebimelech took his family into Moab (the previous enemy conquered by Ehud) and there they perished except for Naomi, Boaz remained in the land and flourished as a *"man of wealth"* who was faithful to the Lord. It seems to show us that one doesn't need to follow the majority and more than that, **should not** follow the majority, since they are usually wrong. The standards of Christian conduct should never be dictated by the mores of the world, or even by those of carnal believers. God gives us a rule of conduct and clear guidelines to lead us in a pathway of consistent faithfulness to Him under all circumstances of our lives. We also learn from that example, that choosing the apparently easier pathway as did Elimelech will result in disaster for a believer, whereas the more difficult choice of obeying the Lord will eventually result in spiritual prosperity and ability to bless others. Which will we choose? The results make this choice very important!

Jabin and Sisera

We have noticed the origin of Canaan, going back to Ham as his forefather, and have seen that this was one of the evil nations that God was determined to judge through His people. Judah had gone with Simeon and had fought with the Canaanites in Judges 1, but we also have noticed that Canaan's power was not overcome (1:29-30, 32-33) and here we find a resurgence of its efforts. In this case, Canaan is being led by Jabin, the king who dwelt in Hazor.

It is notable that we find the same nation and the same-named king in Joshua 11:1. This one is not the same king; perhaps it was a title of the ruler, but it suggests that this principle comes up once and yet again. Jabin means "intelligent," or "he will understand" (Jackson, Hitchcock), and this suggests an exaltation of man's wisdom rather than dependence on God's. If this links with the period of church history represented by Pergamos, we can see the correlation. That period of compromise with the world that allowed the same world and its thinking to penetrate and be accepted in the church was surely marked by a display of man's wisdom. It seemed right, and surely it resulted in a lessened persecution because of the favour now received from the world under the emperor Constantine. However, the end result was a further step downward in declension away from the truth of God and faithfulness to Him.

Hazor is suggestive in that it means "an enclosure, a village" (Gesenius), and is not this indicative of the desire of man for security that can be obtained by association with others providing mutual protection? Under the protective wing of the government of Rome, more departure took place, even though there were faithful men who stood for the truth. In such an environment, a clear, uncompromising expression of one's convictions is more difficult than when we are separate and identified with God alone, even though such a stand may cost more.

Jabin had a captain over his army named Sisera ("battle-array," Gesenius) who dwelled at Harosheth of the Gentiles. Harosheth seems to be identified with a location presently called Tell el-Harbej, on the south bank of the Kishon River at the foot of Mt. Carmel, and some thirty miles southwest of Hazor (*Distressing Days of the Judges*, Leon Wood). Harosheth seems to mean "carving, engraving, workmanship" (Gesenius, Jackson), and these together suggest the activity of the world in its wisdom to set itself against the truth of God in active warfare.

This was the period of church history when great attempts were made by the enemy to rob the church of precious and essential truths by false teachings. Some of these were Arianism (attack on the deity of Christ), Appollinarianism (attack on the true humanity of Christ), and Nestorianism (making our Lord two persons). These errors had to be combated by faithful men in that day, men such as Athanasius and others. These heresies represented the intelligence of men apart from the wisdom of God, and they would have resulted in ruin to the church. Thankfully, they were combated and refused by the majority.

Linked with that warfare was the workmanship of men that can seem so attractive to the carnal believer, the artifices of those who would add to the simplicity of God's Word and thus take away from its spiritual power. Is this not what took place during the time represented by Pergamos and moving into Thyatira? Wasn't it during that time that the use of vestments, incense, processionals, infant baptism, and predominance of the clergy (*"doctrine of the Nicolaitanes,"* Rev. 2:15), began to become accepted and assumed a recognized place among the church along with many erroneous practices? The Lord also refers to those who *"hold the doctrine of Balaam"* (Rev. 2:14), and it was his instigation that caused the breakdown of separation between God's people and the Moabites, bringing God's judgment on both. All this could be developed further, but it seems clear that Canaan has a parallel spiritually with the world system that would embrace and amalgamate with itself all that which is supposed to be purely and solely for Christ.

This oppression by Jabin over Israel caused them to cry unto the Lord. This was a proper response, but it was also the result of the severity of the oppression. We would cry also, if we were oppressed by the overwhelming power of an enemy who had 900 chariots of iron! However, if there had been proper exercise of soul on their part resulting in their maintaining the desired relationship with the Lord, they would not have been crying to God for deliverance now. Do we learn from this? Carelessness in our associations and relationships with the world along with accommodation to the desires of the flesh ultimately result in our finally awakening to the realization of how far we have gotten away. However, even then, the cry of God's people is always heard by Him who knows and sees all, and in their acknowledged weakness and dependence on God, room is provided for God to come in to deliver them from their enemy. We will see that deliverance in the next chapter.

7

Third Recovery Under Deborah and Barak
Thyatira and Man's Weakness
Fourth Enemy: Midian and Amalek

This phase of the history of God's earthly people is very interesting in many ways. One interesting aspect is the instrumentality of women to bring about deliverance. Chapter 4 begins with Deborah, a woman judge and prophetess who motivated Barak to respond to God's call. It ends with Jael, the wife of Heber the Kenite, ending the life of Israel's terrible enemy, Sisera. Deborah was a prophetess while Jael was a pilgrim. Both possessed the character that believers need to overcome enemies, such as receptiveness to the Word of God and living in separation from this world.

It is generally true in God's Word, that women typify at least three things: weakness among the saints, the maternal nature that longs for children in the faith, and devotedness of heart that is expressed in faithfulness to the Lord and His Word. Regarding the weakness among saints, it seems that when women are seen in a prominent place, it indicates weakness of leadership by men, who should have been taking the lead to rule and deliver the people of God.

This period was, without doubt, a time of great weakness but God would work, despite that weakness, to deliver His people because they had cried to Him in their desire and dependence. Barak, in this chapter, appears as a weak, vacillating man who refuses to go to the battle against Israel's enemy without Deborah going with him. On the other hand, that desire for her company was good, in that he recognized his own weakness and the need to depend on her, the one who had the voice of God and could speak with divine authority. Often God will use others to accomplish His purposes even though those who should take that responsibility refuse or fail to do so. God is not limited in His use of instruments.

However, as Deborah told Barak in chapter 4:9, the result of his reticence to respond would be that the honour of victory would be given to another. (However, Barak and not Deborah is mentioned among the heroes of Hebrews 11). Certainly this is a word to brethren who have responsibility among the saints! If we do not respond to that responsibility, the result will be the ultimate loss of honour and reward from God, now and in the day of review. There are brethren whose voice is never heard in the assembly, who never participate in a public way, and yet they would very adamantly be against women taking part publicly, and rightly so. However, when we abdicate our responsibility, we are only encouraging actions that are contrary to the teaching of God's Word, and the results that may follow would be our responsibility.

We see her maternal character regarding God's people in her song, where she speaks of herself as *"a mother in Israel,"* (5:7) and she looks at Israel as one assessing their qualities and commitments, either expressed or lacking. We always need those, whether brethren or sisters, who have a great concern for the welfare of God's people and long to see spiritual development in each one.

Deborah also displays the character of a devoted believer when we see how she approved the evidences of devotion that some of Israel displayed in response to the call for battle. She has much to say about the heart and how they responded: *"the people willingly offered themselves,"* (5:2); *"My heart is toward the governors of Israel, that offered themselves willingly among the people"* (5:9). She notices the *"great thoughts of heart"* and the *"great searchings of heart"* (5:15-16) that Reuben displayed. One would surmise that she was a spiritual woman who expressed a great depth of devotion to the Lord in her life and service for Him.

Links with Thyatira

We link this phase of Israel's history with that of the church as depicted in the letter to the assembly in Thyatira (Rev. 2). In

that case, in a way similar to Deborah, a woman is in prominence, though she is a very different kind of woman in her
character, practices, influence and results. Jezebel was a woman
who sought to control her husband, King Ahab, and she was
the instigator of many of his evil deeds. In the letter to Thyatira,
we see her as the one behind the terrible practices that had entered to defile the saints and corrupt the assembly.

She is also called a *"prophetess,"* though never raised by God
(Rev. 2:20), and she was using that position to teach practices
that were contrary to God's Word. Clearly she was out of her
place in an assembly, for God never gave a place of prominence
to a woman in an assembly. This is not due to "Paul's bias against
women," as it is sometimes said, but it is God's order clearly
taught in His Word, even though the majority of Christendom
refuses to acknowledge it. Could Jezebel's prominence be due
to the failure of brethren in that assembly to fulfill their own
responsibility, and thus they had caused weakness that allowed
this condition to take place? This is not stated, but it seems in
that case, as in this story in Judges, that her prominence and
influence no doubt resulted from the failure of men to lead the
saints as they should have.

When we think of the state of church history that this period
represents, we can see that many things were out of place in
the Roman Catholic system that rose to power, including giving a woman (Mary) prominence that God never intended her
to take. Other evils came in as well, including an amalgama-
tion with the world that tolerated the moral evils that abounded
in that religious system. Going on to the end of this section in
Judges, we see that it closes with the song of Deborah exalting
the exploits of two women. In this case it was well-deserved,
but it was not what ought to have been. Without going into further details of that sad letter to the assembly in Thyatira, we
will confine ourselves to what we can learn from the history of
Deborah and Barak.

Deborah's Place and Work

Many things are interesting to note with regard to Deborah.
We see that while she was a prophetess, God's Word does not

indicate that she was one who God had raised, as were those in the past. In Judges 5:7, she says that *"I arose a mother in Israel."* Perhaps this indicates that her taking this place was not God's original mind, but it was the result of her recognizing a need that existed and her willingness to fill the gap.

Her being a prophetess indicates that she was in touch with God and He was communicating His Word to the people through her. It is also evident that she had the confidence of the people, since *"the children of Israel came up to her for judgment"* (4:5). This is always essential in anyone who would minister righteousness among God's people. David said, *"He that ruleth over men must be just, ruling in the fear of God"* (2 Sam. 23:3). As a judge (4:5), she would apply the truth that she knew from God's Word to the cases that were presented. More than that, her name ("her speaking" or "eloquent") seems linked with her giving an oracle from God. It was during a time of weakness and oppression by this cruel enemy (Jabin) when God would raise deliverance through one who knew God and who was able to communicate God's Word to His people.

Many methods may be sought and utilized by brethren when they see difficulties and bad tendencies among the saints, but what is really needed is the Word of God in its power, brought to God's people by one who is in touch with God and dwelling in a place of fellowship with Him. Human expedients and methods may seem to bring about change and improvements, but nothing will work a lasting result like the power of God's Word applied in its simplicity.

Deborah, though functioning in the place of the man, was still one who clearly recognized and acknowledged the principle of headship (Gen. 3:16; 1 Cor. 11:3); she is seen in relation to her husband, Lapidoth, whose name means "lamps, firebrands." F. W. Grant indicates that his name suggests the power of the Holy Spirit on the Day of Pentecost, when there appeared cloven tongues as of fire resting on their heads at the coming of the Holy Spirit. Together, they suggest God's Word functioning in spiritual power to work effectively among the saints, resulting in deliverance and restoration. In addition, she was dwelling under the palm tree, a place suggesting spiritual prosperity and peacefulness. It was to Elim that Israel came after the waters of Marah, which were bitter. At Elim, with its 70 palm trees and 12 wells of water, Israel found rest and refreshment along the journey. So here, in the midst of the strife and oppression, is Deborah, living in peaceful contentment and communion with God. The palm is also linked with righteousness (Ps. 92:12). Palm trees were found in the sanctuary of Solomon's temple and in the temple that Ezekiel saw as well (Ezek. 41:18). Thus, this picture indicates a believer who is enjoying the nearness of God's presence and living in the power of that union of fellowship with God.

We see, also, that her location was between Ramah ("the high place") and Bethel ("house of God"). Ramah suggests our position in the heavenlies (Eph. 1:3), linked with Christ and seated in a secure place before God while Bethel speaks of our relationship with the saints in testimony in this world under the Lord's authority in His house. These two relationships should characterize every child of God as they indicate where we are before God and where we are in this world. If we are moving in genuine assurance of our position secured by and in Christ, then we should also be living in the good of a beneficial relationship and fellowship with the saints in this world. This is a place where one lives who possesses the potential to be used of God to deliver His saints! No wonder the children of Israel came up to her for judgment. No doubt they recognized that she could give them God's mind to resolve difficulties. May the Lord continue to raise up those among the saints today who could fulfill a similar function, bringing peace and deliverance to God's people in the midst of adversity and trouble!

Deborah and Barak's Call

Two things mark Deborah in addition to her work to judge the people. Those two things are her encouragement of Barak and her song in chapter 5. We will look at her song later, but at this point we will look at her work to stir Barak and give him God's commandment to obey. Barak's name means "lightning" and this suggests the swiftness and power of God's hand to deliver His people from their distress and to vanquish their enemy.

Is it not true, that often we feel that God doesn't hear the cries of His people and is slow to move to deliver them from their adversity? Yet when it is God's time, His work can and will be done in His own way. God is not tardy to fulfill His Word and make good His promises (2 Pet. 3:9), and His *"hand is not shortened that it cannot save; neither His ear heavy that it cannot hear"* (Isa. 59:1). Barak was the son of Abinoam ("father of pleasantness, or grace") so he was a proper instrument to be used for their deliverance. He lived in Kadesh-naphtali, "sanctuary of the wrestler," and we remember the experience of Jacob in Genesis 32 where as a result of his nocturnal encounter with God, his name was changed to Israel. Jacob's wrestling with God had to come to an end, his own strength broken, before he could receive spiritual power and his name be changed. Barak suggests a man who seems to possess the potential of power to be used for God under divine control and direction, one who will be engaged in wrestling with an enemy and overcoming through God's power. He is one who has spiritual energy that can be directed and used for the blessing of the Lord's people and the honour of Christ. In this sense, it is good that he recognized his own weakness and need for one who had a direct relationship with God and could communicate the Word of God to him. Deborah is a picture to us of an overcomer who is able to communicate something of that divine strength to others to encourage them.

Deborah called Barak and gave him a command from God that was clear, personal, and explicit. He received instructions regarding who would be involved in this battle for deliverance. They were the ones who were nearest at hand and who the enemy's invasion had most severely affected. Those who are far off and do not realize the impact of the enemy's work do not usually fight. Rather, those who have suffered under its effect are most exercised to resist oppression.

God has His men to use in every crisis, and while there were those of Ephraim in the time of Gideon who were not called (8:1) and others refused to participate (8:6, 8), God's command at this point specified who would be included. Gideon also had to see the majority of his 10,000 men go home, and they may have felt deprived in that they were not able to go to the war, but that was God's way and He selected His men. We may not always be included in the number of those who are called upon to do exploits for God, but we can and should rejoice in what is being accomplished for God and for His people. As the hymn writer has penned it, "Leave to His sovereign sway, to choose and to command" (C. Wesley Gerhardt, "Put Thou Thy Trust in God," *Believers Hymnbook*). What is important is to respond and go when God calls, to be ready and available for whatever task is according to His will, and thus to be in a useful condition for God.

Barak's Reluctance

It is remarkable that, under the conditions of God's specific call and Deborah's communication of what God would do with the promise of certain victory, Barak refused to go unless she went with him. Her language seems to indicate that God had already called him to do this, (4:6) but he had refused to respond up to this point. So God used a woman to stir him again, to instill in his soul a needed confidence so as to cause him to move.

Perhaps there are many brethren who know that God has called them to a work, either in the local assembly or in a wider sphere, but they are not willing to move from their position that is so comfortable and tranquil. What an account will need to be given to God in the day when all is judged in His presence! Perhaps a sister will need to speak to one like this to stir him to obey God's call and begin to work for Him. Whatever is needed, God can accomplish it, as this case shows.

An Overwhelming Foe

As God's people, we are engaged in a spiritual warfare with an enemy who seems to have an overwhelming display of power. Sisera had a vast array of men in his army with 900 chariots of iron, and against him came Barak and Deborah, with only 10,000 men to oppose him. There wasn't much in favour of their paltry force and on the face of it, the "odds" seemed overwhelmingly against them! Later, God would do something even far greater by the hand of Gideon in the next section, delivering the people with a small group of only 300 men! Doesn't this emphasize that victory doesn't come as a result of natural power or ability, but through the power of God? Remember what Elisha told his servant? *"Fear not: for they that be with us are more than they that be with them"* (2 Kgs. 6:16). We recall the words of John's epistle, *"Greater is he that is in you than he that is in the world"* (1 Jn. 4:4). We could consider many other passages for our encouragement, but we have a precious truth, as one passage descriptively puts it, that in our spiritual warfare, *"we wrestle not against flesh and blood...wherefore, take unto you the whole armor of God"* (Eph. 6:12-13). God arranges the entire matter so that it would be evident that the victory was gained, not by carnal or physical might nor ability, but rather by the power of God working on their behalf. *"Not by might, nor by power, but by my spirit, saith the LORD of hosts"* (Zech. 4:6).

Barak's Victory

It is nice to see that Deborah always recognized and acknowledged that victory would only come from the Lord. In verse 14, it was the Lord that went out before Israel to defeat Sisera and it was *"this day"* that He would accomplish that victory. What else could Barak do, or what should he do, except move forward to face a foe that had already been defeated? We have already noticed this principle: we are not victorious over spiritual foes in the Christian life by our own natural ability or power. On the contrary, usually one who has great natural ability is the least likely to depend on God, and thus he is the weakest. May we learn to lean on God for every resource which we need in order to overcome and emerge victorious in our spiritual warfare!

Not much needs to be said about the battle; God's Word doesn't record much detail. The language of Judges 5:20-21 indicates that heaven fought against Sisera. Not only that, but it seems that God sent a storm that resulted in a flood that swept them away, for *"the river of Kishon swept them away, that ancient river, the river Kishon."* Josephus records in his "Antiquities of the Jews,"

> "There came down from heaven a great storm, with
> a vast quantity of rain and hail, and the wind blew the

rain in the face of the Canaanites, and so darkened their eyes, that their arrows and slings were of no advantage to them, nor would the coldness of the air permit the soldiers to make use of their swords; while this storm did not so much incommode the Israelites, because it came in their backs. They also took such courage, upon the apprehension that God was assisting them, that they fell upon the very midst of their enemies, and slew a great number of them; so that some of them fell by the Israelites, some fell by their own horses, which were put into disorder, and not a few were killed by their own chariots."

Something of this kind of event is intimated by Deborah in her song (Judg. 5:4), where we read *"LORD, when thou wentest out of Seir… the clouds also dropped water."* Also in Judges 5:20 this is suggested, and was accompanied or followed by a slaughter. It seems that the God-sent storm caused a flood of water from the River Kishon that mired and overwhelmed the chariots of Sisera so that they were helpless against Barak's army. This caused great disorientation among the troops and resulted in their overthrow. We read, *"Then were the horsehoofs broken by the means of the pransings* [tramplings, or plungings] *the pransings of their mighty ones"* (Judg. 5:22). This indicates that the horses broke their harnesses and galloped away from the battle. Do we not see how this indicates to us that God Himself is against the powers of darkness and forces of evil? Of course, we know this intuitively, but we need to remember that, while evil seems to reign and opposition to Christ prevails, God still moves in active warfare against all elements contrary to His purposes and will ultimately bring about their defeat.

Jael's Decisive Act

The defeat of Sisera was a foregone conclusion, and though he tried to escape on foot, God was not done with him yet. The final blow would be lodged by the hammer and tent peg of another woman, Jael, in her own tent. We learn from verse 11, that her husband's family was related to the Israelites through Moses, who, as we know, was the great deliverer of God's people. Heber means "fellowship" or "comrade" but it was a fellowship of those who were separated, as the verse indicates. Jael lived as a nomad, or a pilgrim, with her husband, without being identified with any earthly place apart from the location of their tents.

We learn in 1:16 that the Kenites had come out of the city of palm trees (location of Jericho) and lived among the Israelites. They seemed to be favourably attached to the nation, though never part of it entirely and were finally represented in Jeremiah's day by the sons of the Rechabites. In that instance in Jeremiah 35, their separation was expressed by abstinence from strong drink or wine due to their obedience to the command of a long-departed father. Their adherence to the mandate of a deceased ancestor was a rebuke to Israel as it displayed a marked contrast to their disobedience to God and His Word. They maintained that characteristic of separation in obedience to a man while Israel failed in separation from the nations through their disobedience to God.

Separation Important

Separation is a valuable principle and a very important characteristic of life for God's people. Many shun the thought of genuine separation unto the Lord. They know that this would require a degree of devotion to Him that would involve avoiding the elements of the world that the flesh desires but which are abhorrent to the Lord. Speak about separation to some, and they think only of what they could not do if they were to obey the Lord in that way. They want their worldly pursuits, entertainment, activities and intermingling in the empty occupations of the unsaved. On the contrary, separation is a most valuable position to take, always resulting in increased power with God, more genuine fellowship with God, and greater usefulness to God.

Sisera, using the normal wisdom of the world, thought he could flee away in safety from the battle as a common foot soldier, using his wits to elude capture and death. He fled to the tent of Jael. Their tent was located not far from where Barak had lived, in the *"plain* [oak] *of Zaanaim, which is by Kedesh."* It is interesting that Heber had separated himself from the Kenites and pitched his tent in the area where Sisera would eventually be seeking to flee, no doubt with God behind the scenes.

One wonders why Heber would be separated from the Kenites and yet be at peace with the king of Hazor; we might marvel that there would be any relationship at all between them, but such was the condition during those days of weakness. Yet what Heber had done may not have been the mind-set of Jael with regard to these enemies of Israel. It is also possible that the treaty of peace with Jabin did not go so far as to embrace Sisera and his particular Canaanites. More than that, it seems that she recognized a higher claim, and that was the need for a relationship with the people of God, and not with their enemies. Thus, in her case, another link needed to be severed, so she took up that exercise to express her absolute fidelity to the Lord and His people. She acted in a manner that removed every element of compromise with God's enemies. In this way, she imitated God's dealing with those priests who offered *"strange fire"* in Leviticus 10:1. She also acted in a similar way as Rahab (Josh. 2), when she sheltered Israel's spies in Jericho and aligned herself with God's people against her city and nation. A crisis of this nature calls for and displays the depth of conviction in one's heart regarding the things of God.

Her act typically shows one's personal opposition to doctrinal error as well as the destruction of Amalek, or moral error, both of which will destroy the saints. She had the Lord's mind in stopping His enemies by destroying Sisera, a leader against God's people. She is an example to us and a warning against the danger of not taking a stand against every element that is contrary to the things of God. We see a spiritual fulfillment of this in the admonition of John the elder to the elect lady in 3 John. She was to refuse all fellowship with those who would come with a wisdom that was contrary to the doctrine she had learned, so she turned them away and did not allow them into her house. This is using the tent peg of a separated life that rejects all that is associated with evil, whether it is doctrinal or moral.

Wisdom of the World

Sisera represents the wisdom of this world that rises up in opposition to the wisdom of God. This was part of the problem that had crept into the assembly in Corinth and which Paul contends against in 1 Corinthians 1:17-2:16. It is a problem that can and does exist in our day, when the world's reasoning begins to dominate and control the direction and activities of God's people. It is a mode of reasoning that leaves God out of the parameters that are used to reach any decision. This reasoning begins and ends with man and his desires. Sisera reasoned that he would find safety in her tent, claiming the normal exercise of eastern hospitality and security. Who would think of searching for him in a woman's tent? And if she stood at the tent door and told anyone pursuing him that no one was there, would he not be safe? Surely, if man alone was involved, that might have been the case. But God was against Him (5:20) and his supposed place of safety became the place of his death.

There is a sense that there is a Sisera in every one of us. This enemy can creep into our life so easily and adapt himself to the things that we like, with the result that it seems cruel or very difficult to deal with it. However, like Jael, it is our responsibility to do so, carrying out that act of self-judgment that is essential for our preservation and deliverance. It is so easy to compromise with an enemy that seems so adaptable and so willing to find itself at home right where we are. Yet, having come so close, it calls for judgment on self so that we might be preserved from condemnation with the world (1 Cor. 11:32).

Jael's Tent Peg

Jael did not know how to use a sword and didn't attempt to do so. Barak used a sword, but she knew how to use the hammer and tent peg. Any nomad, moving constantly and living in tents, would be aware of the importance of the tent peg to secure a safe place in which to live. We see in her a picture of a believer who uses the things he or she knows how to handle, not aspiring to use materials to which they are unaccustomed. Shamgar didn't use a sword either; he used an ox goad, a tool that he was familiar with and could handle properly. We all have a certain area of expertise in the truths of God's Word that we are capable of using to overcome the foe. It may not be the flashing sword of conquest, but even a tent peg can be used to gain a victory. One might not be able to preach, nor be allowed to do so. However, there is power in the simple testimony of a separated life upheld by one placing confidence in God daily, putting into practice the truths of God's Word and proving them to be effective. David would not go to fight Goliath in Saul's armour, and that was not due to a difference in size. It was because he had not proved it, and did not know how to fight with that equipment on. He used what he had proven for himself through God's power when he had delivered the sheep from the lion and the bear.

Jael waited until Sisera was sound asleep, then she went softly and applied the force of the hammer to drive the tent peg through his temples right into the ground. If Sisera represents man's wisdom operating against God's wisdom, then we see that it is characterized by wrong thoughts that must be defeated, or put to death. She used the tent peg, representing the believer's pilgrim character. But she also needed the hammer, and this reminds us of the power of the Word of God to give force to this character to overcome.

Do we not need to defeat wrong thoughts, those aspirations of men that exalt themselves against the knowledge of God? Think of 2 Corinthians 10:4-5: *"For the weapons of our warfare are not carnal, but mighty through God to the pulling down of strong holds; Casting down imaginations, and every high thing that exalteth itself against the knowledge of God, and bringing into captivity every thought to the obedience of Christ."* Paul was using the tent peg of truth in relation to the believer's pilgrim character to vanquish the opposing wisdom of the world. This was true as he dealt with the problems in Corinth as well as in his disputing with the unsaved. Again, he combats that kind of wisdom in 1 Corinthians 1:19 and 2:4-8, which was causing so much difficulty among the saints in Corinth. We need to be able to oppose and defeat the false reasonings of the world in which we live, a kind of thinking that seems so attractive and right to men but which is diametrically opposed to the mind of God. It is only from the standpoint of one who, like Jael and Rahab, takes a stand on God's side in his rejection of a world system, who will defeat the wrong thinking that can invade and affect the people of God.

Sisera and Jabin were subdued under God's hand working through the sword of Barak and the tent peg of Jael. What a blessing that deliverance was! Verse 24 tells us that *"the hand of the children of Israel prospered, and prevailed against Jabin the king of Canaan, until they had destroyed Jabin king of Canaan."* With the defeat of Sisera and the army, Barak went on to deal with the source of the problem, which was the king of Canaan in Hazor. The victory was complete, but remember, it began and ended with a woman, those who in weakness and in their own place, were being used of God to bring about deliverance to His people. You and I, in all our weakness, can also be used by God if we are yielded and willing to do His will.

Deborah's Song (Judg. 5)

It seems notable that the songs of women in the Bible celebrate divine victories over Satanic power. Notice the song of Miriam in Exodus 15:20-21 and the song of the women in 1 Samuel 18:6-7 that celebrated David's victory over Goliath. This is the only song in Judges, so it has a high level of importance attached to it. Deborah joined with Barak to sing of God's victory over the forces of Canaan, and this song is a picture to some degree of the assessment of our service at the judgment seat of Christ. Here men are assessed according to what they did or did not do to help accomplish God's purpose in this case. It is solemn to think of the day when our actual deeds will be manifested in the Lord's presence and we will be judged, not according to what we thought we would do or planned to do; rather it will be on the basis of what we have actually done. See 1 Corinthians 3:13-15. Our minds go to the parables that relate to this principle in the Gospels, such as Luke 19:12-27, where we see the results of service during the nobleman's absence. It may be that many saints, thinking that one day they will become involved in the Lord's work, never actually engage themselves in any meaningful activity in the things that really matter for eternity. One has said that at the judgment seat of Christ, no one will receive any reward simply for having been a successful businessman in this world, or having gained a high reputation in any sector of society, nor for simply being a person well-liked by others. It is the work that is done for Christ according to the standard of God's Word that will merit a "well-done" in that day.

Deborah's song is divinely recorded as part of inspiration; however, that does not mean that every part of it was spoken by inspiration of God. It is a production of a victorious, yet failing person, and it records the exultation of the victor over the defeated foe. In the first part of the song, it seems that possibly Deborah is exalting her own position and exploits when she seems to indicate that no one else had accomplished what she had. In verse 6, she seems to be saying that Shamgar had not accomplished a victory for Israel, neither had Jael. It was not until she arose. Note that she does not say that God raised her. So there is some measure of personal pride in what she has accomplished. Whether this is actually what she intended or not, it is not commendable for anyone who has been used of God, to have an attitude that gives the impression that they are the "only one" or that it was through their own exercise or ability that this came to pass. Self-exaltation is always a dangerous thing, but we more readily judge it in others than in ourselves!

Praise to Some

Then we mark that she noted and commended those who participated in the Lord's battle. In verse 2, we learn that *"the people willingly offered themselves."* While there are difficulties in the translation of this expression (JND translates it as *"that leaders led in Israel"*), it is evident that those who served are being recognized. Again we read about, *"the governors of Israel, that offered themselves willingly among the people"* (v. 9). We notice that here, as in the days of the building of the tabernacle, what she recognized is the free will of the saints to participate and sacrifice what they are and have. This is the kind of service that God will accept and acknowledge. It is the kind of response that **should** arise from our hearts. If there is not a willingness to do His will and devote all to Him, it suggests a serious problem of the heart.

Praise to God

Above all, she offers praise to God for His delivering power. Those who are prominent (v. 10) and those who have been delivered (v. 11) will recognize that God has been their deliverer and that He has accomplished this work righteously. Songs of the saints would always have this ultimate purpose, would they not? We praise our God, for it is He who has done all things well. Nothing could be accomplished apart from His work, the expression of His grace and His power. He is the One who is due all the praise and honour, and He will have it, both now and in the future. We sing at times,

> Praise our God, Who willed it thus,
> Praise the Lamb, Who died for us;
> Praise the Father through the Son,
> Who so vast a work has done.
> —John Cennick, "Brethren, Let Us Join to Bless,"
> *Believer's Hymn Book.*

Those Who Failed and Those Who Came

Then, in the second part of the song, we learn about those who failed to respond to the call and those who did come. There was no actual indifference to God's battle; we learn in verses 14-15a of those who fought. Ephraim acted, apparently, to forestall any attempt by Amalek to take advantage of the battle to rob God's people. Do we not need those, who can recognize that other enemies of the saints will try to use a conflict to cause further ruin and loss among the saints? Amalek, representing the work of Satan through the flesh, would always attack those who are weaker, the "hindmost" of God's people. Ephraim rendered a great service in this regard and she commends them for their vigilance.

We learn that Benjamin, Issachar, Manasseh (Machir) and Zebulun were with Barak, though not mentioned in the previous chapter. Do we not learn that there are some who are involved in service for God who may not be recognized until all is manifested at the judgment seat of Christ? Not all exploits are evident or rewarded in this life; we wait for the assessment of the righteous Judge (1 Tim. 5:24-25). What is also noticeable is that some of these tribes were not directly affected by the domination of Canaan, so that they came to the help of their brethren without obligation. It is actually a sin, when believers turn away from involvement in any effort to overcome an enemy or to deliver their brethren from that domination through indifference or apathy. It is too easy to sit back and say that it is "not my problem, so why should I become involved?" God's Word tells us that He will reward those who are exercised to deliver those who have need in this way (Isaiah 58:10-12).

The close of verse 15 turns to consider those who failed to come to the help of their brethren. Reuben, the tribe that should have taken the lead, failed. It seems that they made a start to come, but as one translation reads, *"at the brooks of Reuben were great resolutions of heart"* (Keil & Delitzsch), as if to say that they moved to a certain point, began to discuss the pros and cons of the matter, then made resolutions that they should do something. Then we read, *"Why abodest thou among the sheepfolds, to hear the bleatings of the flocks? For the divisions of Reuben there were great searchings of heart."* It seems that the same thing that caused them to choose to settle on the east side of Jordan, their flocks and herds (Num. 32), now caused them to remain there rather than go to the battle with their brethren. They had done so initially, when they conquered the land, but then they considered their possessions and finally decided not to get involved. They were removed, after all, from the scene of the battle, so they could avoid conflict.

The second expression, *"great searchings of heart,"* is not as strong as the first. It indicates that they had resolutions to do something, but then they sank into mere projects that failed to materialize. Does this speak to any of us, considering that often our concern for material well-being and the desire to "take it easy" overrides any sense of what we ought to do in our service for the Lord? The Lord, speaking about the Sower and the seed, said of the soil with thorns that *"the cares of this world, and the deceitfulness of riches, and the lusts of other things entering in, choke the Word, and it becometh unfruitful"* (Mark 4:19). It seems that this Gospel makes the parable apply to the effect of the Word of God on the believer, and if this is true, the possessions we have can hinder us in our service and faithfulness to God. We need to be careful that this is not the case. *"No man can serve two masters,"* the Lord said, referring to the slavery to material possessions that one can be dominated by (Matt. 6:24). Reuben exemplifies one who has resolves of heart, but due to the love

of ease and prosperity, fails to act and thus comes under repro-
bation by God. Again, we notice that they were judged, not on
their intents and resolves, but rather on the basis of what they
actually did, or didn't do, in this case.

Verse 17 also tells us of others who, in like manner, put their
own safety and commercial activities ahead of the Lord's battles. Dan, in his ships of commercial interests and Asher, in his
place of ease and safety enjoying his comfortable life, had no
heart for any activity for God that would cause them to hazard
life and possessions! This seems too often to be the case today
among us and we should be concerned about this direction of
our lives as well.

Again, reverting to speak of the worthies, verse 18 notes
those who, in an extraordinary way, risked their lives for the
accomplishment of victory. We know, of course, that these two
tribes were the ones chosen by God to join with Barak to lead
the battle. They did not shrink back or avoid the conflict, but led
and conquered; being overcomers, they are recognized here in
the annals of the mighty. How will it be at the judgment seat of
Christ for us?

Verses 19-22 recount the defeat of the enemy kings. They
had come with the expectation of taking a spoil, but they got
nothing for their efforts. God defeated them and they were
overthrown and broken in pieces by His hand.

But then the song turns to others who also failed to come to
help, and Meroz comes under a curse in verse 23. This evidently
was a village that stood in the path of the retreating enemy, but
they declined to become involved and refused to give any help.
It is most solemn to think of some who were so near and so li-
able to be affected by the outcome, yet they would rather leave
the fighting to others and spare themselves. This resulted in a
curse of the angel of the Lord against them, much more serious
than what man might pronounce. Their condition was not seen
as reluctance simply to help God's people, but it is identified as
it truly was, failure to come *"to the help of the Lord."* Refusal or
failure to be involved in a delivering work is identified as refusal to be used of the Lord and that is more serious by far. Let
us be careful that this is not the case for us!

If Meroz is cursed of God, it is in contrast to Jael, who is the blessed one above women (v. 24). To her the honour goes, more than is mentioned for Barak. She merited it, for she accomplished a personal victory that cost her far more than all the rest. Hers was an act of faith despite the element of danger. It was an expression of her confidence in the Lord and her identification with the people of God. The result of this defeat was the expressed sorrow of the mother of Sisera at the fact that he did not return. They had expected victory. Who could defeat such an army with iron chariots? GOD! As a result, the anticipated joy and celebrations were turned into sorrow and loss, the same result that will be true for every enemy that stands against the purposes of God in any day.

As we consider this assessing song, we again think of the relationship between these events and the letter to the church in Thyatira. We note, for example, that the Lord began His appeal to that church by identifying Himself as *"the Son of God, who hath his eyes like a flame of fire, and his feet are like fine brass"* (Rev. 2:18). In other words, He was analyzing their service (v. 19) and discerning what had been done for which He could give His approval. Sadly, like Deborah's song, He noted that there was much to be rejected with great failure. However, also like this song, the Lord recognized those among them who were seeking to be different, *"the rest in Thyatira, as many as have not this doctrine…"* (v. 24). So we see that He always makes a distinction in His analysis of His people. We know that in the system that this church represents, there were (and are), those who overcame the normal, existing conditions and sought to maintain fervent fidelity to the Lord. Out of the Roman Catholic religion came some hymns that express a great depth of spirituality and devotion to the Lord. It would seem that the Lord delights to identify those who rise above the mass of religious confusion and clerical domination to heights of spiritual truth known through His Word. We might ask ourselves if His discerning eye would see in us that willing exercise of heart and action that distinguishes us from the mass of humanity? There is always the promise of victory to the overcomer, and as Barak, Deborah, and Jael overcame this enemy, may we seek to gain the victory over all that would hinder the spiritual prosperity of saints.

The song ends on a note of triumph anticipating the glorious day of His ultimate victory over the forces of this earth that will be gathered against His people again in the future. In like manner, the Lord ends His challenge to Thyatira by moving forward to the day of complete victory, when the coming Lord *"shall rule them with a rod of iron; as the vessels of a potter shall they be broken to shivers..."* (Rev. 2:27). Our minds go to that great valley of Armageddon, far greater than the valley of the river of Kishon, where those united armies of Israel's enemies will be completely overthrown by the Lord. What a victory that will be! Thank God, we are on the winning side now and He will have the praise and honour eternally.

May we learn something from the example of those who fought, and from those who failed. We are writing the book now that will be read farther on and up above. Our actions, or failures to act, in the spiritual conflict are all on record, and in the day of review, all will be manifested, the day shall declare the value of every man's work, and then each one will receive what they are worthy of from the hand of our blessed Lord (1 Cor. 3:13; 4:4-5).

8

Fourth Recovery Under Gideon
Sardis and Partial Restoration
Fifth Enemy: Ammon

The repetition of a sad, doleful comment impresses us when we read this book. Once again, *"the children of Israel did evil in the sight of the Lord"* (Judg. 6:1). Only forty years of rest resulted from Deborah and Barak's delivering work, and God's people had lapsed so quickly into an evil condition again. After such a remarkable deliverance by God's hand, one would think that an extended period of blessing would result, but that was not to be.

We notice that the nature of their evil is not defined in this passage, but typically in Judges, their doing evil primarily refers to their becoming involved in the idolatrous practices of the surrounding nations. This is the character of the first reference to this condition (2:11) and it likely was true during all their history. Of course, we know that idolatry of the nations also involved immorality and evil practices. It is natural for us to think that moral evil is what God hates more than all else, but in reality, **spiritual evil** centered in idolatry is even more serious in God's sight. That is not to say that moral iniquity is not evil before God; we mean that God's order emphasizes what may not seem to be significant to us. The law given by God through Moses began with commandments that were Godward before continuing with the commandments that affected their relations with men. The human heart seems to consider worship of objects apart from the Lord Himself to be of lesser gravity than moral depravity. We find that at the end of this book, Israel never judged Micah's idolatrous house, but in the matter of the brutal murder of the Levite's concubine in Gibeah, the tribe of Benjamin was almost annihilated through extreme severity of judgment. It teaches us that our primary responsibility is to guard our hearts and lives so that the Lord alone enjoys preeminence; the remainder of our behaviour will display proper order if this is the case.

Once again, the Lord delivered them into the hand of one of their enemies. It seems that the affected tribes were mainly those in the northern part of Israel and included Manasseh, Zebulun, Asher and Naphtali (6:35). In this case, the enemy was Midian (with Amalek, 6:3), and Israel served Midian seven years.

Midian's Origin and Character

Midian was a nation that was related to Israel through its origin, having descended from Lot through one of his daughters (Gen. 25:2). The name means "strife" (Brown, Driver, Briggs, Fausset, Smith). They were also linked with the nation of Moab many times in their history (Num. 22:4; 25:6; 25:17) as well as by birth. Midian's father (Ammon) was Moab's brother by birth (Gen. 19:37-38). Midian seems to have been primarily nomadic by nature while Moab was a nation more settled. They were quite rich through what they had gained by trading or even by plundering others when possible. In this chapter, we find that this was their practice (6:3-6) so much that they impoverished Israel by their raids at this time. It seems that they routinely raided the rich produce of the Esdraelon Plain (Valley of Jezreel, Judges 6:33) in the central area of the land of Israel during the time of harvest and deprived the Israelites of their food.

The meaning of their name and their activity suggest those sad occasions when strife comes in among God's people. Those times always result in spiritual starvation among the saints. Midian, being a kindred nation to Israel, shows us that the strife can come from those who are near by, even related, and who have some things common with God's people. In the spiritual realm, this is even sadder than opposition that comes from without. Such fighting and dissension among the saints results in their impoverishment. The ruin caused by Midian was only a precursor to that which Abimelech caused in chapter 9. That was clearly a case of fighting among the children of Israel, causing more serious harm than Midian. We also see more of this fighting at the end of the book when the tribes went to war against the tribe of Benjamin. This kind of action can happen on a local level with disastrous results. It happened in a larger sphere during church history, when there was division between churches with one seeking to have power over others. Paul warns the believers, *"But if ye bite and devour one another, take heed that ye be not consumed one of another"* (Gal. 5:15).

Think of the division that existed in the assembly in Corinth,

> *"Now I beseech you, brethren, by the name of our Lord Jesus Christ, that ye all speak the same thing, and that there be no divisions among you; but that ye be perfectly joined together in the same mind and in the same judgment. For it hath been declared unto me of you, my brethren, by them which are of the house of Chloe, that there are contentions among you. Now this I say, that every one of you saith, I am of Paul; and I of Apollos; and I of Cephas; and I of Christ. Is Christ divided? was Paul crucified for you? or were ye baptized in the name of Paul?... Now in this that I declare unto you I praise you not, that ye come together not for the better, but for the worse. For first of all, when ye come together in the church, I hear that there be divisions among you; and I partly believe it"* (1 Cor. 1:10-11; 11:17-19).

James warns the saints about fightings between the saints in James 4:1-4, and in all these cases, it seems to have been caused by departure in heart from the Lord resulting in a certain kind of spiritual idolatry being practiced. In an interesting way, F. C. Jennings (*Judges and Ruth*) links the three nations that are found together in this place with the verse cited above: *"From whence come wars and fighting* [Midian] *among you? Come they not hence, even of your lusts that war in your members* [Amalek]; *Ye adulteresses, know ye not that the friendship of the world* [Moab] *is enmity with God?"* There is a great deal of truth in that application!

No doubt this condition was (and is) due to a personal lack of subjection to the Lordship of Christ. In the larger sphere, it resulted from failure on the part of church leaders to understand the principle and practice of the sovereign control of Christ over

His church (Eph. 4:1-6; Col. 1:18; Rev. 1:16; 3:1). It also comes from the idea, still perpetuated, that churches should form into groups or denominational systems. The teaching of God's Word emphasizes the autonomy of the local assembly and the fact that each individual assembly, though linked with others because of spiritual fellowship enjoyed, is directly responsible to the Lord of the churches and not to some earthly head. The New Testament teaches nothing in addition to the existence of local assemblies that are responsible to the Lord.

However, we find Paul prophetically warning the Ephesian elders in Acts 20:28-30 that *"after my departing shall grievous wolves enter in among you, not sparing the flock. Also of your own selves shall men arise, speaking perverse things, to draw away disciples after them."* His prophetic view proved to be true very shortly, as church history attests. None of us are immune from this tendency of seeking to be *"lords over God's heritage"* (1 Pet. 5:3), so Paul's warning is fitting, *"watch and remember"* (Acts 20:31).

Link with Sardis

Admittedly, the correlation of conditions described in Judges and those seen in the seven churches of Revelation 2-3 is not perfectly clear. This is also true in other suggested links between the church periods addressed in those chapters and other passages, including the parables of the kingdom of heaven in Matthew 13, comparison with some kings of Judah and Israel, etc.

However, without wanting to "push" this aspect too far, there are enough indications of similar conditions so that we have linked this period and condition with that which the Lord addresses in His letter to Sardis in Revelation 3:1-6 and to that period of church history that Sardis represents. Following the period of Roman Catholic domination (Thyatira), with its strife, preeminence of a woman, confusion, and bondage of saints to men with their political intrigues and conflicts, God raised up exercised men who were like Gideon, men such as Martin Luther, John Calvin and Zwingli, along with others, to bring deliverance to His people. The Protestant Reformation, so called because of the protests of these faithful men against the abuses in the Roman Catholic religion, began in the early 1500's and was led by men such as Martin Luther.

In Sardis, the Lord presents Himself as the one who has *"the seven Spirits of God and the seven stars"* (Rev. 3:1). He is the One who exercises sovereign control over His church and over those who, like the stars, bear responsibility to guide in the dark night of its experience. His desire is to have His people subject to His sovereign control and not dominated by men who fit the characteristic of having *"a name that thou livest, and art dead"* (Rev. 3:1).

Sardis seems to refer to the entire Protestant system that resulted from that great movement of God called the Reformation. We see that, like God's work under Gideon, He raised up men who, though conscious of their own weakness, acted for God and in dependence on God to bring deliverance. However, this sadly only resulted in those and other men seeking to use political power to control what men believed and practiced, and this would be seen typically in the abominable conditions that resulted after Gideon's death under Abimelech's domination (Judg. 9). The Lord says to the church, *"I have not found thy works perfect before God"* (Rev. 3:2). Another translation indicates that the Lord is saying that in His sight, no works were perfect before God. This was the case in the Reformation, and it has resulted in men, as always, falling short of the divine ideal and failing to respond perfectly to the desires of God's heart. The fragmented state of Christendom today is only the result of men failing to return entirely to the basic principles of God's Word with subjection to divine authority.

However, the Lord also identifies among them in Sardis, a few faithful ones who he describes as *"a few names even in Sardis which have not defiled their garments"* (Rev. 3:4). Jotham would correspond with those who are identified as overcomers and who refused to be dominated by man's rule as seen in Abimelech (Judg. 9). During and following the Reformation period, there were those who stood apart from the state church system and who sought to remain faithful to the truths of God's Word and show loyalty to the Lord in belief and practice. These included those persecuted believers identified as "Anabaptists" and others who were also fiercely persecuted and martyred by those in the "Protestant" camp, even as they had been by the Roman Catholic system. This condition of persecution and offense connected with faithfulness to the Lord has not changed, and no doubt, it will always be true until the Lord comes.

Again, directly referring this part of Israel's history in Judges 6-9 to the time of the reformation, we think of the strife, wars and fighting that existed during that period. Time and space doesn't allow a more complete consideration of the intrigues of the Roman Catholic system, fighting between the popes and the political powers, and the conflicts that also existed between the different parties of the reformation. It makes sad reading, considering what God intended to accomplish to bring deliverance to His people, but which fell so far short due to man's failure. It was a period of conflict that robbed God's people of their peace and prevented them from enjoying spiritual food and prosperity. We think of the Thirty Year War in Europe that had such a devastating effect on the populace, the wars in Bohemia, campaigns against the Albigenses, the Waldenses and other faithful believers, along with the inquisitions that resulted in many martyrs for the faith of Christ. Certainly it was a time of strife, conflict and confusion that arose from man's greed for power and possessions derived from innocent men. The divisions among "Protestants" that exist today began, in part, at that early stage, and they continue to cause strife and division among God's people.

However, like Jotham and others in Israel (Judg. 9), the Lord recognizes and promises reward for the overcomers. He says that though they are despised and rejected presently, there will be a day of honour in the presence of the Father in heaven (Rev. 3:5). Their character of purity and fidelity to the Lord in life that was the cause of their suffering will then be expressed in the *"white raiment,"* and though driven out from among men and not permitted the recognition that was due to them, He says that *"I will not blot out his name out of the book of life."* Heaven's record of those who were severely afflicted for their faithfulness to the Lord will be revealed in the day of His glory. *"Then shall every man have praise of God"* (1 Cor. 4:5).

Midian's Impact on Israel

Midian did not seek to destroy Israel; they only robbed them of all their crops and sustenance so that they were impoverished (6:6). In Judges 6:7-10, God used a prophet to remind them of the reason for their condition; it was due to their disobedience to His Word. He was the first prophet sent to Israel during the time of the Judges, so his message was of vital importance. God was seeking to warn His people so that they might realize the basic cause of their distress. It was, as usual, their disobedience to His Word and unfaithfulness to His person.

Whenever there is disobedience in our lives, there will be strife in our relationships with other saints. This strife will always rob the saints of their tranquility and spiritual food; they won't receive the solid teaching of God's Word nor will they be able to rest in the green pastures (Ps. 23). One has said that one of the very important functions of an elder is to provide and maintain peace among the saints in an assembly. This is verified by God's shepherding work toward His people described in Ezekiel 34:15, *"I will feed my flock and I will cause them to lie down."* God knows how important these peaceful conditions are among the saints, and no doubt, the devil knows it too, since he seeks to do all he can to sow discord among the brethren. May the Lord help us to be on guard against this tendency by *"endeavoring to keep the unity of the Spirit in the bond of peace"* (Eph. 4:3).

Sadly, Israel's resulting condition was worse than what they had ever experienced in their history. First of all, they were forced into hiding in dens and caves, living without the light upon them. This suggests that in their rejection of the light from God, they found themselves in the depths of darkness and poverty, a condition that is always the result of not *"walking in the light"* (1 Jn. 1:6-7). In addition, God sent a prophet to speak to them rather than speaking directly (1:2) or through an angel (2:1). This indicates their distance from God, yet the prophet's coming also suggests God's mercy, that He had not totally abandoned them. In the third place, we notice the challenge the Lord brings them consisting of seven elements, all of them concerning what God had done for them, manifold demonstrations of His mercy and His power; yet, *"ye have not obeyed my voice"* (v. 10).

The cause of their condition was laid at their own feet. God had warned them long before, yet they failed to heed the warning that would have been the proper response to God's mercies. Let us always ask ourselves if this might be the condition that we experience through our own failure: loss of light, felt distance from God, and the challenge of God that causes an awareness of our own failure.

Gideon: An Overcomer in Poverty and Strife

It is always good to see a believer thriving and going on despite adversity. We can see other instances of this characteristic; one exemplary individual is Boaz who, at the end of the period of famine, was a *"mighty man of wealth"* (Ruth 2:1). Believers can either succumb to the surrounding straitened conditions, or they can rise above them, mounting *"up with wings as eagles"* (Isa. 40:31). They can accomplish this through waiting on the Lord, that is, depending on Him to give strength to accomplish all that is necessary through them.

When we first see Gideon, he is a man who was threshing wheat. We learn that the man God is going to use to restore food to His people is one who is exercised to get food personally. Other translations tell us that he was threshing wheat *"in"* the winepress. Evidently the Lord is telling us that the winepress was not being used for its intended purpose. Wine speaks of joy and the fruit of the vine indicates the fullness of God's blessing to His people. There was no joy among Israel under these conditions of strife and poverty. There may not have been joy, but Gideon was determined to secure something of the blessings of the land for himself, no matter what might be the condition of others. A lesson we can learn from this is, if your heart is not joyful because of problems and difficulties, do what is within your power and get food for your soul. Joy will come in its time when deliverance has been accomplished.

Do we not learn from Gideon that a believer cannot properly blame others for the lack of spiritual food? God has placed us in a land of spiritual plenty ("the heavenlies"), giving us every resource so that we might nourish our souls and feed richly on what He has provided through His Word and in Christ Jesus.

Sometimes we hear saints complain about their circumstances, such as problems that exist in their assembly and the lack of teaching to help them spiritually. Yet, they seem to make no effort to glean for themselves from the same rich and abundant resource that others have to draw from. Gideon's only concern and complaint was in response to the salutation of the angel of the Lord with respect to the prevailing condition of his day. How could this condition coexist with the Lord being with them? His response seems like more than a complaint; it was the voice of perplexity. If the Lord was with them, why was all this happening to them? However, the Lord didn't say, "the Lord is with '**you**,'" but *"the Lord is with **thee**,"* selecting Gideon out from the multitude of Israel. Could we see from this that one who is expressing personal exercise to feed his soul in the midst of strife and famine can know the Lord's presence and experience His blessing?

The Angel of the Lord

The angel identified Gideon as the man who had the Lord with him, but Gideon was thinking of his people and he responds, *"us."* This is a man who can be used to deliver God's people: a man who is feeding himself by exercise and one who is thinking of the welfare of the Lord's people more than his own. This is the kind of spirit that stands in direct contrast with those who were causing their distress, those who were more concerned about self and what they could get than with the condition of the people of God.

The address by the angel of the Lord also indicates that the Lord was anticipating what Gideon **would be** through God's power in his life. He is *"thou mighty man of valor"* (6:12), though there is no indication that he had ever fought a fight nor conquered a foe. He would prove himself to be exactly what God had called him as he submitted himself to God's hand to be used. He manifested the spirit of a mighty man of valour, one who willingly moved against an overwhelming number of the enemy and conquered them. He already was displaying the character of an overcomer when he was threshing wheat in the winepress despite the extremity of the day.

Where Gideon was When Called

We also notice just where Gideon was when God met him. In the elements of the scene, we see a mixture between what speaks of strength and what speaks of weakness. The angel of the Lord (Jehovah Himself) came and sat under an oak, speaking of strength, signifying, possibly for us, the strength that we find in the "tree." It was in Ophrah, a name that means "dusty," and it is not hard to see that the condition of Israel had brought them, and Gideon, into a dry, dusty condition of extreme humiliation. The oak belonged to Joash (indefinite meaning, possibly "despairing one," or "helped by Jehovah"), suggesting the weakness of one who can do nothing without the help of the Lord. He was the Abiezrite, "father of help," and Gideon's name means "cutter down." These all point to him being a man who occupied a place of humility and dependence on God, and this proved to be his characteristic in his service as Israel's deliverer. One would understand that, in any day, it is a very difficult task to deal with strife and division among saints. The only man who can be of help in this situation is a man who is meek, a man who is humble, and one who is depending on the Lord for the strength to accomplish such a great, important task.

God's Estimation of Gideon

We have noted that the Lord's salutation indicates that Gideon was *"a mighty man of valor"* (6:12). These were not empty words, since a man who is thus occupied has the potential to be used of God in a larger sphere. He was not cowering in the caves and dens and saying that all was hopeless and that there was no use trying to do anything. He was doing what he could and he did it effectively so as to gain from it. This character was the Lord's estimation of him at that time, but it was also an indication of what God would make him and how God would use him.

Our strength does not lie in personal ability or might; we must constantly learn and relearn that it is going *"in this thy might"* in order to accomplish anything for God. His might was his dependence on God that came because of knowing his own weakness. The might of God became his own might personally.

It was to be real in his own soul so as to be effective in his life and service for God. Gideon was fully cognizant of his own smallness and incapability as we read his words in verse 15: *"wherewith shall I save Israel? behold, my family is poor in Manasseh, and I am the least in my father's house."* His response seems to indicate that the other members of his family looked down on him, evidently standing alone for the Lord against the worship of Baal, and considered him the least of the family. If this is true, they had little respect for a man seeking to be faithful to the Lord. That attitude has not changed to this day. This response is also much the same as Moses' when God called him (Ex. 3:11). God's answer is always the same, *"Surely I will be with thee"* (Ex. 3:12; Judg. 6:16) and we have the same promise from the same God today, *"I will never leave thee, nor forsake thee"* (Heb. 13:5). This is our strength to overcome and to be a blessing to God's people, and it is a promise that is good right up to the coming of the Lord (Matt. 28:20). Once again we see that confidence in self is a disqualifier for the Lord's service.

Gideon's Hesitation

Yet Gideon desired to be sure that this commission was actually from the Lord, Jehovah. More than once we find him exhibiting a certain degree of hesitation, wanting some kind of vindication and assurance that he could actually depend on the Lord at any particular step. One could criticize him for being a man of "little faith," as the disciples were rebuked by the Lord (Matt. 6:20; 8:36; 14:31; 16:8). However, at the least, like the disciples, he was doing what was right by following the Lord and depending on His power. His little faith did not disqualify him from service. The vital criterion is not the amount of faith that one possesses anyway; it is the possession of genuine faith that makes the person usable in the hand of the Lord (Matt. 17:20). On the other hand, if we were in Gideon's position and were facing such an arduous, dangerous task, we would want to be certain that we had the mind of the Lord and could be sure that He was with us. He needed to know that this was more than a vision or just an impression of his mind, but that the Lord was actually sending him to do battle with the Midianites. He knew the extent of their forces.

Gideon and His Altars

It is noticeable that Gideon began his service for God from the point of three sacrifices, and every sacrifice was entirely for God. He gave the Lord what was due to him, the worship that Israel had deprived the Lord from receiving for many years. He offered a kid with unleavened cakes of flour. It is touching that he would feed the Lord (as did Abraham in Genesis 18) and that the Lord would condescend to "eat" (or receive) what he brought. Of course, we see that his offering speaks figuratively of Christ in His perfect acceptability to God. The kid was the burnt offering, the bread was a meal offering, and the broth expressed the drink offering being poured out. All of these speak of Christ in His sacrificial work to bring about reconciliation between God and man, restoration of a relationship that had been broken by sin. And sin, of course, is what always breaks relationships. It seems that it is only through one's apprehension of the vastness of the work of Christ and its purpose that we can be used of God to see those results applied to the Lord's people when there are "Midianite" conditions existing among us.

The Lord accepted Gideon's sacrifice and demonstrated the reality of that acceptance by causing what he offered to be consumed with fire out of the rock upon which it had been laid. The same typical act of acceptance took place in the life of Manoah and his wife in 13:19-20. Because of the consuming of his sacrifice, Gideon knew it was the Lord speaking to him. The thought of seeing the Lord face to face filled him with reverential fear at the thought, but the Lord's word spoke peace to his soul. In the case of Manoah, it was his wife who possessed the intelligence to calm his fears, but here it was the Lord who spoke to Gideon. We think of others whose fears were stilled by the still, calm voice of their Lord, the One who speaks peace to His people. God's dealings with Gideon were not intended to consume him but rather to strengthen and encourage him.

Then Gideon displayed his positive response to what God had shown him. He built an altar (no mention of a sacrifice upon it). This altar expressed his attitude of worship toward God and his personal willingness to sacrifice himself for the fulfillment of God's purpose. If he had been getting food for himself at the cost involving great difficulty, now he would express his devotion to God in worship and make himself available to the Lord for service as an expression of his fidelity.

More than that, he called the altar "Jehovah-shalom," meaning "Jehovah [is] peace." It means more than "Jehovah send peace," as if he were only anticipating that peace would result from the Lord working for them. It signifies that the Lord Himself is the peace that is needed by His people. All that we need is found in Him, and when He has His rightful place in our lives, then peace will result. It is wonderful to have *"peace with God"* through salvation (Rom. 5:1). It is even more wonderful to have the *"peace of God"* in our souls (Phil. 4:7; Col. 3:15), but how much more to know and have *"the God of peace"* (Heb. 13:20). The people of Israel were longing for peace, but not until Jehovah-shalom had His proper place in their hearts would they have the peace that they longed for. The little expression at the end of Judges 6:24 indicates that this is an abiding principle. It is *"unto this day,"* and even in our lives this is a truth that we need to recognize.

Then Gideon began to receive instructions from the Lord. On the ground of his first feeble responses to the truth that the Lord had manifested to him, he now began to be used as a channel for the Lord to bring blessing to His people. However, notice his first action must be in his own home and where he lived. There was idolatry in his own family and among his people. There was a rival altar and an opposing form of worship that he must eradicate first. This also tested the extent of his obedience to the Lord. Would he act faithfully for God in a place where he would be known and where others would seek to oppose him? He must, if he was to be used of God in any effective way. One cannot begin service for God in a public sphere if he is not being faithful to God in his private life. If one's home is not right, then how can he be effective in God's house (1 Tim. 3:3-4)?

Gideon's First Act

We notice that he must throw down the altar of Baal **before** he can erect an altar to the Lord. The two cannot coexist, though there were those who sought to do so among Israel. *"The Lord*

thy God is a jealous God" (Deut. 6:14-15), and He does not tolerate other gods worshipped alongside Himself. He alone is God,
and there is none beside Him (Isa. 45:6). The Lord said, *"Ye cannot serve God and mammon"* (Matt. 6:24). This is another lesson
that we all need to learn and never forget. The world and its
worship cannot coexist in our hearts with God's worship and
service if God is to use us in any effective way. One must make
a choice and throw down all that stands in opposition to the
Lord. This seems to indicate a violent act, but that is exactly
what the Lord said in Deuteronomy 12:2-3, and it may take violent self-judgment to actually carry out this essential expression
of our fidelity and obedience to Him.

Some would criticize Gideon for carrying out this act at
night. It would seem that he was afraid of men, that he was doing it in a way that would avoid confrontation with others. Possibly, but on the other hand, how could he ever accomplish this
destructive act during the day? Would not the men of the place
oppose him and prevent him from obeying the Lord? We would
take it that Gideon knew the opposition, yet was determined
to act on God's command. He was, in this way, like Joseph of
Arimathaea (John 19:38), who was a secreted (hidden) disciple
in view of the work that the Lord had for Him. If the Jews had
known what Joseph intended to do, they would have done all
to stop him from giving the Lord an honourable burial. Other
passages along with his action clearly indicate that he was not
fearful, nor a secret disciple (Luke 23:51), any more than Nico-
demus was.

Taking ten men (suggestive of the witness of the Law being
fulfilled), Gideon threw down the altar of Baal and cut down
the grove of wooden idols (Asherim) that was by it. These represented the male and female elements of Baal worship, and
both had to be destroyed. He offered the second bullock of sev-
en years upon the altar according to the ordered manner (given
by God). That bullock speaks of Christ as the second Man, the
first order of things having been set aside due to its failure. The
first is always natural, of this world, while the second speaks of
that which is spiritual, from heaven (1 Cor. 15:47; John 3:6). We
see that, as the bullock of seven years, it was identified with the

experiences of God's people. It had lived the entirety of its life under the conditions of Midianite oppression. We learn that the Lord knows the extremities of His people in their every circumstance, as we learn from Hebrews 2:17-18 and 4:15-16. For this reason, He is able to sympathize perfectly with the conditions that we face.

Then, notice that the initiation of God's work to save His people was based on a burnt offering, not a sin offering. This expresses in an interesting way the fact that God's work to display His mercy to His people depends on the knowledge of their full acceptance in Christ, that He has made us *"accepted in the beloved"* (Eph. 1:6). How good it is to realize that our standing before God and His desires toward us are not dependent on what we are or do, but all depends on Christ and what He is and has done for us. They had not confessed sin directly, but they had cried unto the Lord for deliverance (6:6-7), so God would work on His own behalf to accomplish it.

As is always the case, the opposing camp expressed its displeasure with an act of faithfulness to the Lord, but it was silenced by the succinct words of Gideon's father (6:31). That is, if Baal is a god, then let Baal deal with the man who has thrown down his altar. It was not for men to defend him. Of course, Baal was powerless and they knew it, so their mouth was stopped and there was no further objection. As a result of this event, he received the title "Jerubbaal," since he had been victorious in the struggle with Baal, and Baal was proven to be powerless. It reminds us of the great event on Mt. Carmel, when Elijah contended with the forces of Baal and also was victorious by the power of God (1 Kgs. 18). We learn that a child of God, exercised to act faithfully for the Lord's honour against whatever would challenge the Lordship of Christ, will have the joy of seeing every enemy vanquished as a result.

In this act of Gideon, we see a suggestion of the movements of the Holy Spirit during the days of Luther, Calvin, Zwingli and others. It was a time of "cutting down" the idolatrous system that had been erected by the Roman Catholic religion, and it was an act of faithfulness to the Lord and the truth of His Word. It was a time of great fear and trembling, when men went against the existing mode of worship, false though it was. Yet it was a time when such men, guided solely by God's Word and desiring to deliver God's people, were bold to express their readiness to be those who *"hazarded their lives for the Name of our Lord Jesus Christ"* (Acts 15:26) by their acts. We admire them and feel a sense of indebtedness to them; but are there those in our day who are also willing to stand boldly against every element that raises itself against the knowledge of God (2 Cor. 10:5)? They are needed today as well!

Assurance of Gideon's Faith

Now, it appears that Gideon was prepared to move in obedience to God's call. He was not like Barak, who would not go unless Deborah would go with him. No, Gideon has more than that; we read in Judges 6:34 that he was *"clothed with the Spirit of God"* (as we read in the margin of the Newberry Bible and in other translations such as English Standard Version and the Literal Translation by Jay Green). It is as if God said to Gideon, "You feel yourself so weak and insufficient for this task? I will invest you with power by My Spirit and you will be empowered, invincible in battle, and more than sufficient for the task that lies ahead." Would that not be enough to enable any weak believer, sufficient to make one strong in exploits for God? That would be better than "Saul's armour" would have been for David! Well that he refused it, for he had something far better. He could say to Goliath, *"I come to thee in the name of the LORD of hosts, the God of the armies of Israel, whom thou hast defied"* (1 Sam. 17:45). He was clothed with God's power to accomplish an impossible task for God and His people.

Think of Paul's last word to the Ephesian assembly: *"Finally, my brethren, be strong in the Lord, and the power of His might"* (Eph. 6:10). What we always need is the power of God, and many passages from God's Word remind us that while the arm of the flesh and the power of man are vain, there is always more than enough power with God to enable the weakest believer to accomplish great things for God (Ps. 68:11; 108:12; Phil. 4:13). The same power that clothed Gideon is available to us in our service for God today. May we avail ourselves of it in our dependence on God to work!

Leadership in Gideon

We find Gideon calling the northern tribes of Israel to follow him to battle. It was one thing to anticipate going against the Midianites and the Amelekites prior to this point, but now he is committed to action. There are men following him and looking to him for leadership. Is it any wonder that Gideon felt the need to be absolutely sure that he was moving in the mind of God when he called these tribes to warfare? Consider his situation and enter into his thoughts at this particular juncture, realizing that he had not received any direct command from the Lord to call them. This seems to indicate to us that we need to make sure of the Lord's mind at every step of the decision-making process in our lives, especially one of this magnitude of importance.

It would be very easy to criticize Gideon for his request of the Lord concerning the fleece. It is better to see that, as someone has put it, Gideon waited to be fully assured that he was moving in the current of divine sovereignty. It was important to be sure that what he was about to do was not an act of his own emotional state, nor was it from any sense of personal importance. Rather, in view of the coming conflict, he was determined to be sure that this was truly God's will. Great things were at stake and he dared not make a mistake in this action. Twice he asked, and while there is, no doubt, a typical meaning to the dew on the fleece and then on the ground, let us simply notice that it verified to his mind that he could move forward with complete confidence in God.

George Muller expressed the truth that in coming to any decision, what is important is to seek to bring oneself to the point of being willing to move in whatever direction the Lord indicates. Only when we are sure that we are not acting of our own volition can we have assurance that what we are doing is of God and is His will for us at that particular point of time. As a result of this night experience of Gideon (the second of four nights in his life: 6:27, 38, 40; 7:9), he was absolutely prepared for the conflict, and so much so, that he could willingly submit to God's choice and face the swarms of the Midianites with only 300 men.

Who Will Go? Who Will Stay?

Is it not a principle of Scripture, that God often tests His people by very small things, those things that may seem insignificant or inconsequential to us? Those tests determine if we go to the battle for God or if we are sent home. We would all want to be included, no doubt. However, we could be disqualified beforehand by matters that were not considered important enough in our minds, but indeed, they were important to God.

Gideon had 32,000 men (7:3) and one can imagine him looking at them and thinking that possibly he had a chance against the might of Midian, though they were like grasshoppers in the valley for number (7:12). Yet God looked at them differently; He said to Gideon that there were too many (7:2). God was going to win a victory by a method that would not allow men to receive any glory at all. So, Gideon had to send home all that were fearful and afraid. This expressed the truth of the Lord's instruction in Deuteronomy 20:8, *"What man is there that is fearful and faint-hearted? Let him go and return unto his house, lest his brethren's heart faint as well as his heart."* Amazing, isn't it, that there were 22,000 men out of that number who went home? That meant that 69% of his force left at once! They were disqualified because of lack of confidence in God, fearfulness because they were looking at self and not at the Lord of hosts. It is always that way, isn't it? The large percentage of men who went home indicates to us the sense of overwhelming futility that most of Israel felt when they thought about battling Midian. They felt that it was hopeless, so why should they become involved when it would mean nothing but loss? When we look at ourselves, we feel that we can do nothing. We're prone to say, "What's the use, we are so small and helpless. Let's just go home and forget a battle." The result is that we give up before we even start and likely never attempt to do anything for God.

Now Gideon was looking at 10,000 men. Was he thinking that he still had sufficient men to win a battle? Didn't Barak defeat Sisera and the Canaanite army with 10,000 men (4:10)? Surely he could do the same. No, there were still too many men. God was going to do a far greater thing than what He did with Barak. So now the men are given the opportunity to drink from the brook. Notice that Gideon wasn't even told what the criterion of the test would be. He didn't know; only God knew what was being observed from on high. Some evidently stooped down and drank deeply from the brook. That was the natural way, the way they were accustomed to drink in moments of tranquility, without any enemy to fight. What was the natural way of drinking was what disqualified them from the battle. Those who lapped the water that they brought up to their mouths with their hands were the ones chosen for the battle. They were exercising control over what they drank. These were the ones who expressed their consciousness of a warfare that called for alertness on their part. They weren't on vacation or unconcerned about the imminence of the battle. Rather, they were aware of the present danger and consciously prepared to go forward.

Perhaps those who drank deeply of the brook would suggest those who were told in Deuteronomy 20:5-7 that they had to return home from the battle. They had other elements of life, legitimate, no doubt, but because of their occupation with them, they were to go home. These other occupations included having built a house but not having dedicated it, having planted a vineyard but not having eaten of it, or having betrothed a wife but not having taken her. Is it not possible that aspects of our lives that are not settled or put into their proper priority in relation to the eternal can hinder our ability to be engaged in the Lord's battles? How sad to be rejected from service for Him, not because of sin, but because our lives are not devoted entirely to the Lord and His service, with other elements in their proper place!

Do we realize that our little actions, our drinking of the natural streams of life and how we partake of those things that we feel personally necessary are all being weighed and assessed in the divine balance? None of these men were fearful or afraid, so they all wanted to go to the battle. They had confidence in God and eagerness to face the foe. However, how they drank of the water determined if they went or stayed behind.

This also seems to coincide with the teaching of Paul to Timothy in 2 Timothy 2:4, *"No man that warreth* [actively engaged in battle] *entangleth himself with the affairs of this life…"* That is not to say that there is no need to care for the necessary aspects of our life, but it teaches that the primary focus of attention must be the battle in which we are engaged. Distractions can only hinder effective involvement for the Lord.

Is it not true that there are many of the Lord's people with plenty of enthusiasm and confidence along with a strong desire to go work for God? There is no limit on their ability, and gift is evident. However, there may be little things in their lives that are not judged; there are desires and activities that keep them too involved with personal satisfaction and imbibing of worldly elements that will prevent them from being chosen. May we all seek by God's grace to be included and approved in view of being used!

Two groups stood before Gideon. It wasn't his decision that determined which group went with him. Likely he was looking at 9700 men. We all would! But God told him to send them home. Just 300 men to use against an innumerable host of the enemy. That was less than 1% of the original army! Impossible! But, *"with God, all things are possible."* It's sad to think that a vast majority of believers may never engage in any actual conflict against God's enemy. They may be faithful in so many ways, consistent in attending the meetings of the assembly and even participate in some way. Yet excessive involvement in earthly, fleshly, worldly attractions keeps them from being used as God would otherwise desire. What would hinder our lives from being instruments of service or otherwise prevent our engagement in the spiritual battle that rages all around? It would be a terrible loss, when the days of warfare are ended, to stand in our Lord's presence, having allowed trivialities to hinder or prevent us from being used or chosen for God's work.

Victory Accomplished By God's Means

Now Gideon was small enough for God to use him. There was a time in Israel's history when, through overconfidence, they had only sent 3,000 men to fight at Ai (Josh. 7:4). But their overconfidence resulted in a sad defeat, a rout from a small force at that city. In this case, it was not man's overconfidence, but it was God's directive, and there is obviously a vast difference! Yet, knowing Gideon's need for assurance, God graciously gave him a further indication of victory before he engaged in the battle. It is good to remember that the Lord *"knoweth our frame; he remembereth that we are dust"* (Ps. 103:14).

Gideon learned that if there were 22,000 of his men who were fearful without cause, in the camp of Midian, there were many more men who feared with good reason. It only took the recounting of a dream and its interpretation to reinforce Gideon's faith so that he could return to his small band without any fear. The dream (7:13-15), one concerning a barley cake rolling into a tent, suggests the lowliness and humility of Gideon. It was only a cake that would feed the common people, the poor of the land—that was what he was. He began his history by threshing grain for bread, and now he will begin his victory by being reminded that he is only a cake of barley bread. He began by telling the Lord, *"I am the least in my father's house"* (6:15) and now he was reminded of it again. None are too low for the Lord to use, are they? We can easily be like Saul, when God had to tell him that he was too big for God to use any longer (1 Sam. 15:17-19). May the Lord preserve us from being *"high-minded"* (Rom. 11:20).

In this case, we remember, the enemy represents the element of strife and division that can cause problems among the saints. What kind of man can God use in this case? It would have to be a lowly man, one who is conscious of his own smallness and weakness. What kind of weapon would be effective? Previously, the deliverers of Israel had their weapons—a dagger, an ox goad, or a sword. But there was no sword in Gideon's hand, neither in those of his men. Two hands, both filled, one with a torch inside a vessel and the other with a trumpet. (This suggests the principle of consecration, the "filling of the hands for God.") However, these instruments were not of much account as offensive weapons. But when overcoming strife among saints, we don't need swords or daggers in that sense. The spiritually applied Word of God as a *"sharp, two-edged sword"* would be effective (Heb. 4:12; Eph. 6:17), but it must be used in dependence on the Spirit of God. Perhaps swords and daggers are part of the problem. There is a need for a lowly, humble man, leading a small band of men who are united and carrying inoffensive, but effective weapons.

His men acted in unison under his leadership. Gideon was always a man who sought to unify God's people. He could do it, because he was one who always gave a soft answer, a humble response. The wise man said in Proverbs 15:1, *"A soft answer turneth away wrath, but grievous words stir up anger."* His men were following his example and acting under his command. Submission to godly leadership is a key to overcoming strife and division, is it not? He set the example for them to follow, and they obeyed and imitated him in what he did. They were united and God used them.

It may seem foolish to use weapons like these to overcome a strongly-armed enemy. But we think of Paul dealing with division and strife in the assembly in Corinth. How did he do it? He used an argument that seemed foolish to the wise men of the world. It was the preaching (the message, word) of the cross (1 Cor. 1:18). How insignificant in their eyes, but he could declare that *"to us who are saved, it is the power of God."* Then we learn that *"the foolishness of God is wiser than men"* (1 Cor. 1:25), and he reminded them of their beginning, what first brought them salvation and joy in knowing Christ as Savior. In this way he brought them back to the ground of their unity in Christ. Paul was using the lamp in a broken pitcher (making little of himself) and sounding the trumpet of the clear message that had brought about their salvation. He reminded them of something very similar in 2 Corinthians 4:6-7 when he speaks of the light shining out of darkness and the vessel being insignificant in itself. As a vessel, he had brought the light of the truth to them through much suffering and affliction, being conformed to the dying of Jesus, and here he was sounding forth the clarion call of that message to deal with the division and strife that existed in their midst. Certainly, this is the way a humble man, a broken vessel conformed to Christ, would go about reconciling his brethren and delivering them from the evil of this enemy.

We see that for Gideon and his men, there was no battle to be fought. They *"stood every man in his place round about the* camp" (7:21) and the Midianites fought with each other in the ensuing confusion. Now we can see why only 300 men were needed! God was fighting for them, and He caused Midian to fight against themselves. All Gideon and his men had to do was to obey the Lord's command and the Lord did the rest. One could suggest that the enemy of saints, at heart, is fearful; the slightest indication of God's power puts them to flight and God wins a mighty victory. We compare this to David's victory over Goliath and the result among the Philistines; *"when the Philistines saw their champion was dead, they fled"* (1 Sam. 17:51). All depended on one man, and when he was defeated, the rest had no heart for battle.

The Aftermath

Gideon was not a man who kept every aspect of the battle to himself. He included his brethren, others of the children of Israel, as much as possible. We see that he called others, including Ephraim to take part in the final conquest and to share the glory of the victory. This is a mark of a man who can unify the Lord's people. He is not selfish, wanting all the credit for any achievement that has been accomplished. He would include all the Lord's people in the spoils of war. The Lord has done this for us; He has led captivity captive and has given gifts among men, bringing us into a place of honour and acceptance with Him (Eph. 4:8).

However, the attitude of others, such as those of Ephraim, who were not called nor included in the battle at the first, becomes clear at this point. In chapter 12 verse 1, we learn that the same tribe also attacked Jephthah in the same way. It seems that their pride couldn't allow the possibility that they were not given a prominent place in any activity of the nation. However, in contrast to Jephthah, who retaliated against the children of Ephraim and killed his own brethren, Gideon again employed the "soft answer" and as a result, he turned away their wrath. A man that will unite the saints is one who is glad to give the credit to others, even if they were not as completely involved as he was. They had taken the princes of Midian (7:24-25) and Gideon credited them with a greater work than his. Gideon restored unity and removed strife, but sadly, Jephthah produced strife and division among the people. We can do either one or the other, depending on how we respond to the slights and criticisms of others.

Strife and division among the saints is often caused by a desire to get all the credit and by failure to recognize the contribution of our brethren. If we relate this to the days of the reformation, as characterized by Sardis, is it not also true that there was contention on many points and from many sides at that time? We think of the fighting between those who followed Luther and some of those who were called Anabaptists (most of these being faithful believers who refused to take arms to defend themselves). The number of areas of contention between those who were involved in the reformation were numerous and many lost their lives as a result. Those of the Reformation who had "protested" against the abuses of the Roman Catholic system and had based that protest on *"sola scriptura"* (Scripture only) persecuted those who sought to act on the same principle of *"thus saith the Lord."* Depending on the power of the state to enforce their edicts, they killed, oppressed, and persecuted those who believed that only genuine believers in the Lord Jesus Christ should be baptized, not infants. As a result, the movement that began so well ended in a kind of corruption similar to what had been protested against, and it resulted in oppressing all those who disagreed. It is sad to consider how often this kind of rivalry and bitter fighting can ruin a work of God to bring deliverance to His beloved people.

Then Gideon encountered others who were less interested in the defeat of the enemy than his army was. The men of Succoth and Penuel and their princes represent those who refuse to become involved, even refusing to give sustenance to those who were involved in pursuing the enemy. They were not as bad as the princes of Midian who were the avowed enemies of God and His people; these were just indifferent and had no desire to become involved in any way. They expressed their disdain for his army and they made clear their lack of confidence in his ability to achieve victory over the army of the foe. As a result, they came under the discipline that they deserved, in addition to their losing any honour of being participants in the work of God.

There always seem to be those who, while agreeing with the principles of those who are involved in doing the Lord's will, don't want to make the effort that would be needed to obey God's Word themselves. Many believers know and agree with the principles of the local assembly as taught in the New Testament, but they would rather stay in the comfortable places they are accustomed to rather than to *"come ye out from among them, and be ye separate"* (2 Cor. 6:17). As a result, they fail to become identified with those who, with all their confessed failures, seek to be obedient to the Lord's command.

Gideon's Refusal of Kingship

Gideon had displayed honourable qualities throughout his life and service for God. Now he refused, correctly, the honour of becoming Israel's king. In Judges 8:22, the men of Israel not only wanted him to rule over them but they included his sons into the future, so that he would have established a line of kings in Israel. Men would always exalt the one who has been used in a particular way to deliver them, forgetting that it was God who had done the mighty work. There are denominations of Christians today that identify themselves by the name of some great man who has been used of God in the past. This is only a means of dishonouring the name of our Lord Jesus Christ.

A dynasty of kings would also remove the problems that entered their experience between the particular times of each judge, and surely this would be the answer to many of their problems. It is always a tendency to make a man great, looking to him to accomplish what is needed rather than depending on the Lord and His power. As a result, a system of rule and organization is set up that is not taught in God's Word. Gideon was right in his response; the Lord was the one to rule over them.

It is sad that at the close of Judges, we are often reminded that because there was no king in Israel, *"every man did that which was right in his own eyes."* Though Gideon expressed no desire to be their king, he gave his son, Abimelech, a name that meant, "My father is king." Why did Gideon give him that name? Was there some thought lurking within him that secretly longed for that place and authority that he had refused publicly? Whatever was the reason, it is clear from subsequent history that Abimelech wanted to be king and would stop at nothing to achieve that power and position. It is a natural tendency to want power and control over others. This tendency will be seen in its stark clarity when the *"man of sin,"* the Antichrist, takes his place to rule in the widest sphere over men in the future (2 Thess. 2:4). Those who have that ambition always cause great harm to the saints of God and damage the honour of the Lord's name rather than delivering and helping the saints.

Gideon's Last Test

Gideon passed every test triumphantly, except the last one. It is very sad to see a man who had displayed such qualities of humility, dependence on God, and faithfulness fail at the very last. Why would he ask the men for the golden earrings and then make an ephod with them? An ephod was part of the garment of the High Priest, so it seems that Gideon claiming himself a priestly standing. He had refused the kingship, but now he reached for the priesthood. Perhaps the priesthood had fallen into such disrepute at this time that he felt that, since God had spoken to him directly, he could function in this way to receive messages from God to guide the people. In addition, we know that he had offered sacrifices on the altar in the same place where he put the ephod (8:27). Did he intend to continue to function as a priest and then the ephod would be part of that worship? Perhaps it was intended to remind him and Israel of the great victory that God had wrought to deliver His people. Whatever might have been his reason, it is clear that his action was a snare to him and to Israel.

Chronologically, it seems that Micah's house of idols and the false priesthood that he set up in Mt. Ephraim (Judg. 17) had already taken place, since it seems to coincide with events of Judges 2. That would have set a precedent for Gideon, but it was a bad precedent, if that was the case. It was contrary to God's order, placing that office with the family of Aaron, so that making and having an ephod was an empty gesture. In addition, it was contrary to the principle of submission to God's order that had characterized his life to this point. It only teaches us that one may serve well and faithfully his entire life and yet fail at the end. How important it is to walk carefully and to avoid turning aside from the will of God in any way! It also points to the failure of those who were involved in the reformation that had brought deliverance to God's people in that era. There was failure to realize that the divine order was for the priesthood of all believers and the liberty was theirs to function in this way. That violation of the principle of priesthood has resulted in havoc and perpetuation of error in the practices of Christendom to this day. How important it is to follow the clear and simple teaching of God's Word so that testimony for God might be preserved and passed on to future generations in all its faithfulness for their blessing!

The sad commentary at the end of chapter 8 and the sadder story that begins chapter 9 shows the general tendency of the human heart. On Gideon's part, it is a solemn warning of the danger of taking our ease and indulging fleshly desires in the latter stages of life (Judg. 8:29-31). Is it not remarkable that God uses his name "Jerubbaal" at this point? Had he lost his character that had been linked with his victory over God's enemy? Had he overcome (symbolically) strife that caused poverty and suffering only to be overcome by another enemy, that of fleshly ease at the end? God points out that he had *"many wives,"* something that was never the mind of God. More than that, he had a concubine in Shechem. This was only about 6 miles from Ophrah, but she was kept there, separate from the rest of his family. That relationship resulted in a son called Abimelech, whose sad history occupies the next chapter. Perhaps this indicates that after one accomplishes a mighty victory through God and has been used of Him, there can be a "let down" in our guard that results in failure. Then on the part of Israel, we read, *"as soon as Gideon was dead, that the children of Israel turned again, and went a whoring after Baalim, and made Baal-berith* [lord of the covenant] *their god"* (Judg. 8:33). It is as if the children of Israel were only waiting for the day when Gideon would pass off the scene, and almost immediately, they turned again to the idolatry of Baalim worship and forgot the Lord and Gideon. Does it not emphasize to us the fact that when men's eyes are on human leaders rather than on the Lord, their willingness to follow will continue only as long as that leader lives? May the Lord help us to understand and appreciate the fact that the Lord is the Ruler over His people and regardless of the passing of human leaders, He is the One to whom we owe allegiance and must seek to follow faithfully.

May the Lord help us, by way of these few comments on the life and service of Gideon, to learn something of our responsibility to act faithfully for the name of our blessed Lord.

9

Events Following Abimelech
The Man Who Would Be King
Ambition, Contention and Its Results

Ambition of Men

This chapter is one that we wish were not a part of the history of God's people, yet it represents a sad reality that has often been witnessed. The history of the church period as well as our personal experience has taught us that whenever God is doing a work, there will often be some expression of man's personal ambitions, which, through its actions, manifests our tendency toward failure.

Earlier, Paul warned the elders of the Ephesian assembly when he met with them in Miletus, *"For I know this, that after my departing shall grievous wolves enter in among you, not sparing the flock. Also of your own selves shall men arise, speaking perverse things, to draw away disciples after them"* (Acts 20:29-30). It was not long in church history before this actually took place. Men began to arise, seeking positions, exalting one's self over others, forming hierarchies of authority that denied the autonomy of local churches, and thus proved that, in this sense, history repeats itself.

We find in 3 John, that a man named Diotrephes was lording over the saints of the local assembly because he *"loveth to have the preeminence among them"* (v. 9). We learn from 1 Peter 5:3, that elders in an assembly are not to be functioning as *"lords over God's heritage, but being ensamples to the flock."* In Diotrephes' case, as well as that of some others who sought positions of power, there seems to be some doubt concerning the reality of his salvation, but in any case, he was certainly not a spiritual man.

We learn from Jotham's parable of the trees in Judges 9, that the spiritual men do not want a position over others; they are occupied with doing a work that ministers blessing to the saints. They emulate the example of our blessed Lord Jesus as described to us in Philippians 2:3-4. He rightly occupied a position of infinite power and authority, but in lowliness He came down and went continually lower until He endured the cross. We should seek to consider Him and follow His example as believers in our service to God and others. A carnal man or an unsaved man will frequently seek ascendancy over others, and the desire for a position of authority is his ambition.

Application to Sardis

It is both interesting and instructive that the Lord presents himself to the assembly in Sardis as the One who *"hath the seven Spirits of God and the seven stars"* (Rev. 3:1). This seems to indicate that He is asserting His rightful authority and power over those who would represent Him in the churches. He is the only One who holds the stars in His hand. He has the power to raise them up and to make them stand (Rom. 14:14). He possesses all intelligence and knows all the needs of His people. When He raises a man to guide His people, He will give him knowledge and wisdom with grace to minister to their needs and to lead them in paths of righteousness for their spiritual blessing (Ps. 23:3). We see this when God raised David to lead His people, and this is emphasized in Psalm 89:19-21: *"Then thou spakest in vision to thy holy one, and saidst, I have laid help upon one that is mighty; I have exalted one chosen out of the people. I have found David my servant; with my holy oil have I anointed him: With whom my hand shall be established: mine arm also shall strengthen him."*

However, when we survey the events of history, we often see just the opposite condition. We see men wanting to be lords, ruling over others with power and force, even using the might of secular armies and political intrigue to accomplish that end. Millions of faithful believers have suffered and have been martyred under the inquisitions and impositions of power and authority by such men. It is indeed a sad history that has been recounted faithfully in many books, including *Foxe's Book of*

Martyrs, *The Pilgrim Church* by E. H. Broadbent, and *Miller's Church History* by Andrew Miller.

Abimelech's Beginning

This pattern is exemplified in Gideon's son, Abimelech. It is interesting that he was born of the union between Gideon and his concubine who was kept separate from his family, in Shechem. Thus this relationship and this locality became the center of sad and serious problems that resulted because of this son. The man who refused to become king (Judg. 8:23) and rejected the thought of his son becoming king begat a son under questionable circumstances at the latter part of his life (or, at least, the Divine record saves this incident for mention at the point of Gideon's decline and failure).

Does it not seem true that the ascendancy of men to places of power came out of the developing weakness and failure on the part of a previous generation in church history? This is one reason why believers must be exercised to *"walk humbly"* with their God (Mic. 6:8) so as to influence a successive generation to follow their example. What we are in ourselves will inevitably influence for good or ill those who come after us in assembly testimony. Gideon typically combated the spirit of division and strife represented by Midian and delivered the people; however, his son, Abimelech, produced division and strife among the people who had been delivered. We might do the same as he did in our own lives and testimony! One generation of faithful men may build up the testimony for God while the next generation can so easily bring it to ruin! May the Lord stir us to greater exercise in relation to His beloved people!

Abimelech's Ambition

His name seems significant as we learn that Abimelech means "father of a king," or "my father is king." One wonders why Gideon would name his son this, but it seems possible that Abimelech expressed his ambition to begin a line of rulers that would dominate God's people. As we have noted, ambition lurks within most of us! Abimelech's actions illustrate for us the initiation and expression of personal ambition in a man.

Observe what he did: out of his own desires he worked to influence his own (mother's) family, causing them to promote him before the men in Shechem, then with men aligned with him and money used to bribe them, he killed his own brethren. Notice that he had a stronger affinity to his mother's family than to that of his father.

To him pertained a similar propensity as Ishmael, who was a wild and unruly man. Judging from the response that his mother's family seemed to give him, we would say that they represent "carnal" people who are governed by a natural way of thinking. Taking Jotham as representative of Gideon's family, they would typify those who are "spiritual," or a faithful remnant. It is not hard to see that a carnal man can influence those like himself, and then, using their support, seek to destroy those who are of a spiritual character.

Abimelech's appeal to the lords of Shechem and their alacrity in responding to him indicates that among Israel there was a growing desire for a king. Due to their sinfulness, the theocratic rule of God over His people was undesirable to them and seemed unworkable. Indeed, such a form of rule can only prevail either over spiritual persons or by means of force on God's part. It was a **natural appeal** that drew the men of Shechem to Abimelech, for he was their brother. But it was also a **logical appeal**; it made sense to them to have one man rule rather than have a plurality of men ruling over them (9:2). It seems to correspond to the great truth of Proverbs 14:12 and 16:25, *"There is a way that seemeth right unto a man, but the end thereof are the ways of death."* Of course, none of Gideon's sons ever said anything about ruling over God's people! His argument was flawed in that it was based on a presumption concerning something that didn't exist.

Possibly, he assumed that they harbored the same ambitions as he did, but that was not true. However, it sounded good to the men of Shechem and they listened and acted. Don't we see a pattern here that has been continued through the course of Christendom? Men are put into offices or given places of power on the basis of relationship or because of a natural appeal that draws others to support them. In some cases it was due to the strength, abilities and assertiveness of the individuals; perhaps in others, it resulted from the lethargy of men that would rather "have someone else do it." Based on the logical advantage of having one man rule rather than a plurality, gradually the entire system of clergy and laity with the religious hierarchy has evolved. It makes better sense in the minds of many to have one man make the decisions, say the prayers, read the Word, preach the message, and carry out all the functions that should be the responsibility of a plural oversight of an assembly. It is so easy to set aside God's pattern and substitute a system that seems good and that seems to work, is it not? But it is wrong since it is contrary to God's Word and it results in disaster under God's government, as it did in this case in Shechem. God's pattern of Scripture is always right and is always best. We should never forget the principle so clearly expressed in 1 Corinthians 2:14-15. It is only the spiritual man who is willing to receive the things of God, but to other men, the natural or soulish men, those things are foolishness unto them. May God help us to be spiritual men who are willing to follow the principles of God's Word!

Those Who Followed Him

It seems that Abimelech had a large following of men, since in Judges 9:5, he was able to slay all his brethren at one time *"upon one stone."* Was this the same stone upon which Gideon had placed his offering to God at the beginning, the same stone from which the fire came out to consume the flesh and cakes (6:20-21)? He was back to the beginning of his father's work to deliver Israel, but it was a denial of all that his father had done. Gideon had presented an offering to the Lord upon a stone at Ophrah; Abimelech slew his own brethren on a stone, again at Ophrah. It seems like an execution, with the brothers (excepting Jotham) killed one after another by their ambitious half-brother. It would take a reasonable force of men to apprehend and hold, then kill 69 men at one time. But think of the overwhelming force that some men can garner to support them in their desires for power and place among God's people, force that has been used in the past, or even in the present, to incapacitate and kill those who stand in opposition.

The man who has killed his brethren is then crowned king *"by the plain* [oak] *of the pillar that was in Shechem"* (v. 6). How interesting that this was the first place where Abram pitched his tent and built his altar when he came into the land (Gen. 12:6). Such a place was marked by reverential dependence on God and true worship. Here we see a very carnal or ungodly man seeking worship and allegiance from men. Again, we notice in Joshua 24:1, 25-26, that it was under the oak at Shechem where Joshua had raised a great stone to be witness to the covenant the people made with God before he closed his days. It was the place in Judges 7:1, where Gideon had attained his mighty victory over the Midianites. Now, in departure, identified with "the lord of the covenant" or Baal-berith (Judg. 9:4), the location of that evil temple (9:46), their descendents gathered to make his son, an evil man, king. What irony in the stone of Ophrah and the oak of Shechem! How quickly God's people can reject first principles and depart from God's pattern!

All that took place from the beginning of Abimelech's movements never demonstrated the slightest indication of any desire to seek God's will in anything. It seemed right, it "felt right" and all seemed to be good, but sadly, anything done in this way without knowing and obeying the will of God will result in the same end as is recorded here. How important for God's people to be careful to know and obey the will of God, especially as revealed in His Word. The principles of God, whether in Ophrah, in Shechem, or in our own day, never change, and we are responsible to act accordingly.

Jotham's Escape

In his escape, we read that Jotham took his position on the top of Mt. Gerizim, a craggy hill rising on the south side of Shechem to about 800 feet in height and overlooking all those who were gathered in the plain below to make Abimelech king. This was the mount upon which half of Israel had stood to pronounce the blessing of God on His people. The other half of Israel stood on Mt. Ebal, and they pronounced the curse of God upon all those who refused to obey God's word (Deut. 11:30; Josh. 8:30-35). It was this mountain (Gerizim), that was so revered by the Samaritans of later date (John 4:20), where their temple had been reared and where they believed men should worship God. Standing on this mountain, Jotham represents those who seek to be faithful to God's Word and who know God's rich blessing upon them. Clearly, the men aligned with Abimelech speak of those who take their position on a broken law that always brings God's judgment. These men had defiantly done exactly that, and inevitably, God would judge them for their sinfulness. When men set aside God's clear Word and set up their own rules and ordinances, blessing cannot result but only the curse that their actions will bring upon them for disobedience.

It is notable that Jotham was willing to take a position alone in speaking to the men of Shechem. He had narrowly escaped death at the hands of Abimelech's men, so it would be natural for him to flee as far as possible without delay. However, he fearlessly warned the people of what they had done and what would be the result of their sinful behaviour. In this way, he represents a faithful remnant that exists to testify against departure and evil when it rises among God's people. We think of the two witnesses in Revelation 11 who will fearlessly testify for the Lord in the midst of great danger, but with His hand over them to protect them. We applaud such men in other days, but we need them in every period to stand against evil and seek to uphold what is right in the sight of the Lord.

Jotham's Parable

Jotham also has the distinction of being the first man in Scripture to speak by way of a parable. The parable described in clear terms what the people of Shechem were doing and what the results would be. Jotham showed them in his parable (9:7-20) the kind of man who would want to be king and *"reign over* [wave above]*"* the rest. Briefly, he is not a man who can minister any kind of blessing to God's people, nor does he care to. The olive tree, the fig tree, and the vine all expressed their joy in serving both God and man. The bramble had nothing to offer men, but it was willing to receive. The lesson is obvious: the spiritual man is a man who seeks to serve and bring blessing to others, not to assume a position over others. Jotham shows what kind of man Abimelech was, and he prophetically tells the men of Shechem what their end would be.

The **Olive Tree** represents **a spiritual man** who is able to bring blessing to the saints. He can teach them, giving them light (the oil of the lampstand was from the olive) and satisfying their souls. How important this is among the believers, and godly elders will seek to feed, guide and strengthen the saints from God's Word. Having a place and *"being lords over God's heritage"* (1 Pet. 5:3) is the farthest thing from their minds. The bramble has no ability to bring blessing, no fruit, no oil, no help for anyone. But he can "wave over" and take a place of prominence if given the opportunity.

Then he speaks of the **Fig Tree**, a tree that is marked by sweetness and fruit that brings pleasure to man's heart. This tree suggests to us **a fruitful man** in God's assembly, one who is marked by qualities that exemplify the work of the Holy Spirit in his soul to produce a life that is satisfying. However, the bramble produces no fruit, for no one has ever received anything good from a plant like this. A place of authority, with others bowing down and taking a place of submission under him, is what he wants and seeks to gain.

Jotham then turns to the **Vine**, but the vine has no interest in reigning over the trees. It would need to give up its production of wine that cheers God and man in order to do so. This plant represents **a joyful man** among the saints, and his presence is a help and a cheer to the entire assembly. How could he leave that work and give up those qualities in order to take a place of preeminence. Such a thing is the farthest from his mind. But the 'bramble man' is willing to do so, and we notice that he never brings joy but always causes sorrow and suffering.

What kind of believers are we? Are we seeking to do, within our own sphere and God-given abilities, a work that will feed and strengthen, satisfy or bring joy to the saints? If we are engaged in such a work, think of the blessing it brings to the company! How could any believer so occupied consider abandoning that work to take a place over others?

Work of Overseership

We notice that the New Testament clearly teaches us that those who occupy the place as elders or overseers in the local assembly are those who desire a *"work"* (1 Tim. 3:1). It is not a desire to have an office (*"office of a bishop"* in this verse is better translated "overseership"), but an exercise for a very necessary work, a work that makes great demands on those who are properly engaged in it. Many problems have occurred in assemblies when there are men who are grasping after a position and wanting to be an elder "because it is their right," or "because they are better than others," or for any other such reason. It is ideal and scriptural when a man is seeking to do the work out of an exercise of heart for the welfare of the saints and the assembly, and then is recognized as one who is already doing the work.

Jotham describes the bramble as one that is very low, not in its own estimation but in reality. This is a plant that is very near the earth. It offers a shadow to the trees, but the irrationality of the offer is obvious, for the bramble has no shadow. No blessing can be provided by the bramble, but there is an abundance of retributive judgment when it speaks of *"let fire come out of the bramble and devour the cedars of Lebanon"* (Judg. 9:15). No love here! This plant would devour even the trees that are far loftier and greater than it is. This was Abimelech, a man who was lowly, grasping, promising what he couldn't provide, and eventually, destined to be the cause of destruction and death. How sad to see this kind of man among the saints! May God help each of us to discern the true qualities of those who we might recognize in any position of authority over His people.

Church History

Just for a moment, let us briefly mention the relationship between this attitude and that which has been observed in church history. Just reading that sad story of the rise of ecclesiastical systems that resulted in men fighting each other and only seeking to take and not to give, brings cause for concern. When men are more occupied with rising above others and taking a place of power than with feeding and shepherding the saints, it inevitably brings division, rivalries, contentions and ruin to God's people.

We leave it with each person, if interested, to read that history and compare the attitude of the bramble man, Abimelech, with that of others in the past (and present), and then to consider the ruin it has brought. Maybe one might say that those words are too strong; however, we should only consider them in the light of what has happened, compare it with what God's Word teaches, and learn from it. Thankfully, this has not been the attitude nor action of many, but it is of some. What a blessing it is when we read about those who diligently served the Lord and served God's people in the past! Let us heed the exhortation of Hebrews 13:7, 17 to remember them and obey them, those who have and presently exemplify the qualities that are desirable in all the saints of God. God has used these men to preserve local testimonies of His dear people to this present day, and such men will continue to have this positive effect into the future.

God's Governmental Dealings

It was only inevitable that bad feelings and conflict would arise out of an action like this. Those who would begin by slaying brothers will eventually turn on each other. Ambitions and desires for place result in inward tensions and outward conflicts that cause destruction on every hand. We hardly need to spend much time on the remainder of this story, except to notice that another man arose, Gaal (meaning "loathing") who also wanted a place and purposed to dethrone Abimelech. War between them and their parties resulted, and many on both sides of the conflict lost their lives. The city of Shechem was completely destroyed even to the point that Abimelech sowed it with salt (9:45) and those in the tower of Shechem, about 1000 persons, were burned alive. Linking Judges 9:3 and 9:26, we learn that this tower was at least part of the house of Baal-berith, or "lord of the covenant." Their worship of Baal at this point of departure from God had caused them to enter into a covenant with a false king. That covenant had been broken and the people were about to realize the results of evil agreements.

Any person who would contend with his brethren to

achieve a place of authority and prominence needs to anticipate what the end will be. This story is mirrored in the results,
written on the pages of history, of men fighting for prominence
and position among God's people, again with the same sad results. We read in church history of the popes and anti-popes,
contending one against the other. There is record of the days
during and after the Protestant Reformation when well-mean-
ing men used the secular powers of state to eliminate their enemies or suppressed any who disagreed with their position or
practice. This only makes one realize how personal ambitions
can be easily aroused so that sad consequences can result.

Abimelech's End

The end of Abimelech is fitting! While he was in the act of
fighting against his enemies at Thebez, a woman threw an upper millstone (marginal reading) from the tower and it nearly
broke his skull (Judg. 9:53). Rather than suffer the humiliation
of having a woman cause his death, he commanded his armour
bearer to take his life instead, which he did. How interesting
that it was a woman, Jael, who also dispatched an enemy of
God's people by driving a tent peg through the temples of his
head (Judg. 4:21). This act again reminds us that the problem
in these cases stems from wrong thoughts and attitudes in the
individuals responsible. However, those who, like these wom-
en, act on God's behalf out of devotion to Him, even though in
weakness, can accomplish a great work that will bring peace to
the people of God. More than condemning wrong thoughts in
others, we should, first of all, use the effectively-working Word
of God to cast down high thoughts and reasonings in ourselves
(2 Cor. 10:4-5), so that we will not cause problems of the same
nature among believers.

10

Fifth Recovery Under Jephthah
Philadelphia and More Weakness; Disunity
Sixth Enemy: The Philistines

After Abimelech died, Tola ("a worm") and Jair ("He will enlighten," or "enlightener") defended Israel (Judg. 10:1-5). Once again, we encounter men who the LORD raised up to defend (save) His people and who did so without much being recorded of their lives. These are called minor judges, but that is only in the sense that little is recorded of them, and they evidently were not involved in great accomplishments against the enemy. We can only say that God has men who, when they are raised to a work (not a position) by Him, can produce conditions of peace and tranquility, even though their work may not appear to be so startling or outwardly evident.

God recorded the useful service of these two judges who preserved the nation for 45 years (if their years are combined; they may have served concurrently). We might seek to learn from them that it is a great work for God to maintain the testimony for the LORD, even though there might not be much to record. We need those in every day of the church's testimony who are exercised to fulfill the work that God has called them to do.

Tola as Judge

Tola's name suggests that he represents a man who was a contrast with Abimelech. In his name ("a worm"), we discern the character of a man who was like our blessed Lord, meek and lowly. A man like this can counteract the devastation and ruin resulting from a man (Abimelech) who wanted place and power. His father was Puah, a name of uncertain meaning but which means, according to some, "utterance". Dodo ("beloved") was his grandfather, so that we sense the influence of a man who acted in lowliness by depending on God's Word and knowing a close relationship with God. This type of man could preserve the LORD's people during those troubled times.

Tola was of the tribe of Issachar, but he served as judge in Ephraim. It is possible that this was because the tribe of Issachar had not fully settled in the area assigned to them at this point; they were still scattered through the other tribes of the area. (Issachar's designated possessions were to the north of Ephraim.) Yet it is clear that Tola had influence among those where he was living and he provided wise and effective leadership in troubled times.

We can only surmise the conditions in that area following the tumult of Abimelech's rule, so a judge who could maintain peaceful conditions was very valuable. It is always good to see a faithful brother who is a "peacemaker" (Matt. 5:9), one who can provide such conditions for the recovery and preservation of the people of God.

Jair's Judgeship

Then our attention turns to Jair. His name means "enlightener" ("witness," or "testimony"). It is possible that his period of work was coincidental with that of Tola; they served God and His people on opposite sides of the Jordan. We particularly notice that Jair was a Gileadite (10:3). From this, we note that the focus of the book's activity has shifted to the area east of Jordan with the result that the judge who followed him in the divine record was Jephthah, also a Gileadite. This is the first time that the book mentions a judge from this area. Being farther from the center of Canaanite worship of Baal, it may be that the effect of evil worship had just begun to affect that side of Jordan.

God raised up a man at the right time to use him to preserve and deliver His people. God meets the need at the required time. It seems that his work continued what Tola began, though in a different area, so that Israel enjoyed this unusual type of deliverance for a prolonged period. Men who act in humble dependence on God and effectively use His Word will always have this effect on the saints. It is sad when this is not the case.

These tribes lived further from the central area of the purposed inheritance in the land. They had chosen to settle on the east side of the Jordan because of favourable conditions existing there (Num. 32). We learn that choosing attractive places for flocks and herds (material possessions) does not deliver people from problems and oppression by the enemy. Normally it is the place where we encounter more problems. We can observe a vivid example of this in Lot's choice when he separated from Abram (Gen. 13). He, like the 2½ tribes of Israel, made his choice based entirely on physical attractiveness and economic enhancement. A pathway that seems right and good to us may be exactly the one that will place us in the most danger and expose us to the fiercest attacks of the foe. However, God did not leave them to themselves, even in this location; He raised judges and saviours to deliver them and Jair was one of them.

Jair had 30 sons riding on 30 ass colts who occupied 30 cities. There are two thoughts that are worthy of our consideration in this seemingly unimportant statement. One is, as Leon Woods has put it in *Distressing Days of the Judges*, that it seems to indicate a tendency toward a kingly lifestyle. To have such a large family indicates that he had many wives, which was the manner of the eastern monarchs of that day. In addition, his control over 30 cities through his sons seems to indicate that he was exerting a dominating power in the area. It would be normal, after Abimelech, for the people to continue to desire some kind of king, and this tendency continued until God finally gave them Saul.

On the other hand, he was evidently an able man, and he served in a manner that God approved of. In addition, he was sharing his responsibility with others who were of his own nature and who had an influence that reached farther than his own. He was not one to concentrate all power into his own hands and act dictatorially. Riding on ass's colts indicates their peaceful purpose, and as they had an effect over 30 cities, it must have been for the benefit of all who were included. This is always an important principle to observe; government in an assembly or among God's people is not reserved for one man; God intends that a plurality of men will fulfill that responsibility. This is a safeguard against dictatorial rule, such as Diotrephes exercised in the assembly where Gaius was (3 John). Plurality of government in any assembly is a necessity.

Departure Once Again

The record of the positive influence of these two judges covers only five verses. Then we read, for the sixth time, that the children of Israel did evil in the Lord's sight and began to serve the gods of the nations around them. Not only that, but they also forsook the Lord and served Him not. In the overview that is found in Judges 2:12-13, we read that they forsook the Lord God of their fathers, but this is the first time that this departure is directly linked with a period of their history.

This result is inevitable, because doing evil and departing from the worship of the Lord is essentially forsaking the Lord to become identified with other gods. *"Ye cannot serve God and mammon,"* said the Lord in Matthew 6:24. The Lord tells us that He is a jealous God (Ex. 20:5 and 5 other references) and will not share His honour with another. Paul could say to the Corinthian believers, *"Do we provoke the Lord to jealousy? Are we stronger than he?"* (1 Cor. 10:22). Their involvement in activities connected with the idol's temple was a means of doing so, even though they did not realize it.

Sold unto Ammonites

As a result, in Judges, the Lord sold them into the hand of the Philistines and the children of Ammon. Israel, we read had been serving (worshipping) the gods of the Philistines and the Ammonites, along with other gods of the nations around them (Judg. 10:6-7). As a result, the Lord delivered them into the hand of the same people with whose gods they had identified themselves. These nations vexed and oppressed those who lived on the east side of the Jordan for eighteen years.

It is interesting that the extent of their oppression was so great! The Philistines lived on the west side of Israel's inheritance but they joined Ammon to vex the Israelites who lived on the east side of the land. In addition, Ammon, who lived to the east, also crossed over Jordan to oppress those of Israel who lived on the west side of Jordan (10:8-9).

Forsaking the LORD seems to lead to widespread and extreme vexation by the enemies of the LORD's people. What we may do in our own departure and sinfulness also seems to have a wider effect on the entire number of the saints. Note the truth of Hebrews 12:15, *"Looking diligently lest any man fail of the grace of God; lest any root of bitterness springing up trouble you, and thereby* **many** *be defiled."* This is a truth that we see in the case of Achan in Joshua 7. It is very important to seek to live carefully, constantly realizing that our actions will influence the lives of others who also belong to the Lord. This means that we should and must be exercised to maintain faithfulness in ourselves regarding our own lives.

We suggest that the Ammonites typify the rationalization of man's natural thinking as it would intrude into the realm of the spiritual. The Corinthian believers were evidently reverting to this kind of reasoning and bringing it into the assembly (1 Cor. 1:17-2:8). As a result, Paul reminds them that it was the simple preaching of the message of the cross that had reached them and blessed them, for they were not naturally great, noble or wise.

The Philistines, as we know, represent the impact of religious men who claim "Christian" ground, but who have never known the redemptive value of the work of Christ personally. They were in the land, but had "wandered" there (meaning of the name), and had never passed through the experiences of Israel that typify the pathway of a soul in salvation. These are two great enemies of the saints in every day, and departure from simple dependence on the Lord and His Word will always result in domination by these two elements.

Confession and Repentance

The resulting distress of God's people was so great that it caused them to confess their sin (Judg. 10:10, 15), even to the extreme extent of casting themselves unreservedly on God's mercy (10:15). Sinful departure of saints is never good, but if it results in their coming to genuine repentance to cause them to recognize that all they can do is to depend on the mercy of God, then it will have a lasting effect. They knew that their condition was their own fault and as a result, they could plead nothing else that could deserve anything good from God's hand.

Paul commends the saints of the assembly in Corinth for their *"sorrow according to God"* (2 Cor. 7:8-11, margin of the Newberry Bible) that resulted in a genuine change in their behaviour and attitude. They became willing to submit to the truth that Paul had expressed and, as a result, they carried out the actions that were necessary. We see a picture of this in the response of Israel during this time of trial in their history.

Having come to this point before God, He would not leave them without a deliverer to express His mercy toward them. Though the LORD had said that he would deliver them no more (10:13), no doubt that statement was intended to test the depth and reality of their repentance, for it grieved the LORD to see their misery (v. 16). Our God always is a merciful God, One whose heart longs to bring blessing and restoration to His people when they truly repent (2 Chron. 7:14).

However, their deliverance required further humbling of the nation (at least those of Israel who lived in the area of Gilead). God was going to use a man that they had previously driven out of their midst because of their jealousy and hatred (Judg. 11:1-2) to bring about their deliverance. It must have been humbling for them to send for Jephthah at this time after showing such animosity toward him. Yet it was part of God's design to use a rejected man to bring about their deliverance.

We remember that the One who will bring eventual deliverance to Israel because of their future repentance is the same One who *"was despised and rejected from among men."* The despised Man will be exalted and received by Israel without reservation in that day (Isa. 53:3-5; Zech. 12:10-14).

Jephthah's Beginning

Notice that Jephthah did not have a good beginning. He was the son of a harlot, a sinful union with his father that resulted in his birth. In that respect, his birth was on a lower level than that of Abimelech, who was the son of a concubine. However you might read verse 1, it does not appear that his father dealt very honourably with his wife or his family. Of course, that bad beginning was not Jephthah's fault! He was reaping the results of what his father had done, and he experienced the reaction of the vicious hearts of his brethren. Perhaps they were acting out of selfishness, not wanting to share the inheritance with a half-brother who had this bad reputation from birth.

Whatever might have been their reasons, Jephthah was thrust out and then went away to the land of Tob. It teaches us that whatever we sow in our wrong behaviour will be reaped eventually, though the attitude of Jephthah's family was deplorable. If they were refusing to share their father's inheritance with this son of their father's illicit relationship, it only manifested a spirit of selfishness that would keep everything for self.

Underlying many actions and reactions toward other brethren in Christ may be a spirit of resentment, selfishness or exclusiveness that results in divisions and disharmony. We need to judge our own spirits in relation to any act that may seem, on the surface, to be justified. It may only be a cloak for our own wrong desires.

Suggestions of Philadelphia

Since we are relating this book to the periods of church testimony and what the Lord says to the churches in Revelation 2-3, we need to consider how this relates in some faint way to the next assembly, Philadelphia. We might recoil at associating Jephthah with Philadelphia, and it is true that we can only make vague and incomplete suggestions at best. This is sometimes true regarding Old Testament pictures of New Testament truths.

Jephthah, at his best, was a very strange man; he was a mixture of what was spiritual and what was carnal, or fleshly. He rises above Abimelech, in that he had desires for God and appreciated his need of God's power. He also was willing to fulfill promises made to God, even though he seems to have acted in a certain measure of ignorance towards divine truth or of God's holy character. However, in some of these ways, he can represent those of this church period who were commended by the Lord and not reproached as others were, yet were far from perfect. We would acknowledge that this is true of all of us. Is it not evident, that while differing measures of spiritual exercise exist among us, there also can be found a certain measure of carnality, or walking according to the flesh, in all of us as well? We know that even the best of men are only men at the best! Moreover, is it not true that we also did not have the best of beginnings? In addition, would we not acknowledge that the world and natural relations would reject any believer who has any character of Philadelphia about him or her?

Looking at Revelation 3:7-13 and what the Lord writes to the assembly in Philadelphia, we learn certain things that correspond with the story of Jephthah. We learn, for instance, that it is the Lord who opens the door in His own time, and this door provides an opportunity for His people's service (3:7). Clearly, it was the Lord who opened the way for Jephthah to come from exile to lead the people to battle.

Then we also note there was a synagogue of Satan that opposed these believers (3:9), but the Lord would make those of that synagogue to come and worship at the feet of these humble believers. In the changed attitude of his brethren toward Jephthah, we see a suggestion of this same alteration and learn how God can bring about a similar change of heart to exalt His own despised people in His own time.

Just as Philadelphia, Jephthah had only a little strength in that he exhibited no character that would have given him a place of leadership among Israel. His strength was in the Lord, who had prepared and brought him to that place. We also see that the result of Jephthah's victory was jealousy by Ephraim that resulted in conflict between brethren rather than unity. We also cannot avoid noticing that Jephthah's men expressed a certain form of legality in their dealings with the Ephraimites that resulted in them slaying quite a number of them at the crossing.

All this has its application to conditions that we would rather not think about with reference to the possible condition of the saints typified by Philadelphia, but we should acknowledge it, even though it is not very appealing. It represents a tendency toward legalism that sadly has been seen in the history of the recovery of truth, a legalism that would impose stringent requirements on others and judge them severely, without love or grace, on those grounds. Even in days of recovery of truth and with the exercise to carry it out through faithfulness to God, elements of behaviour can exist that are contrary to the high ground that we profess to hold.

Jephthah's Preparation

Jephthah gained a name for himself as a *"mighty man of valor"* (11:1) through personal victories during his rejection. We recall that the angel of the Lord so called Gideon (6:12) before he had engaged in any battles. Jephthah had attracted a following of men so that he became qualified as a leader. These men are assumed to not have had a high standing, since they are described as "vain men" or men without a purpose. However, Clarke says, "The word may, however, mean in this place poor persons, without property, and without employment. The versions in general consider them as plunderers."

We remember that similar men followed Abimelech (9:4), but in this case, these men were not making war against their own fellows but against the enemies. Perhaps there is a difference (and the word is not used), but David was identified with men who in some respects were similar when he was in the wilderness (1 Sam. 22:2). It seems possible that Jephthah and his men had a higher character than empty persons expressed; Leon Wood has suggested, in *Distressing Days of the Judges*, that

> "He and his band probably operated more in the manner of David and his group years later, protecting cities and settlements from marauders. Particularly in this day of Ammonite incursion, much of this protection likely was involved with occasions when the Ammonites made strikes into the land areas north of Gilead."

While Jephthah's circumstances were not the best, God was preparing him for the work that he would yet accomplish through him. He was in Tob, a name that means "good," located not far away, so that he was available and accessible when the time came that Israel needed his services. He still maintained as close a relationship with them as possible, despite the conditions of his rejection.

Israel's Cry to God and Appeal to Jephthah

The attacks of Ammon seem to have predominated in this case and now they were intensified (11:4) to the extent that the Israelites became desperate for deliverance. The elders of Gilead made the 80 mile round trip themselves to appeal to Jephthah to emphasize the importance and authority of their appeal.

Jephthah's response to their appeal seems to express two things. One is that he showed his continuing resentment toward the way they had treated him, not the entire nation, but those who were his own relatives. Jephthah was evidently not a man who could or would forget past insults and abuse. Retaining resentments and holding grudges against brethren can be a source of division and problems. What they did to him cannot be excused, but he would have been a better man if he had left their wrong in the past and refused to dwell on it. Our lives are too short, and the work we should be doing is too great, that we should permit ourselves to nurse attitudes such as this, but, sadly, at times it is the case.

However, it also seems that it was a further means of God's humbling the nation so that they were forcibly reminded of their past behaviour. To seek the aid of a rejected man and to be reminded of their commitment to make that deliverer their head (10:18; 11:8) would further remind them of their weakened condition and how desperate they were. Therefore, they promise to make him their head (captain) over them. His language seems to indicate that some of his brothers were now occupying that position of authority in Gilead (11:7).

Jephthah could be criticized for seeking a commitment from them that they would give him that place. However, he was going to represent the nation in his dealings with Ammon, and it was only in that capacity as their leader that he could adequately do so. It suggests to us that God intends that deliverance by Christ is to establish His headship and authority over those delivered; we remember that Christ's work for our salvation is to have the intended result that we, as believers in Him, willingly submit to His authority.

Jephthah's Manner

It is remarkable that Jephthah began by seeking to negotiate with the Ammonites. Keeping in mind that he was a man of war and had been more accustomed to fighting than discussing, it is most unusual. In addition, the normal pattern for one who has been brought back to fight the enemy, especially by those who have despised him in the past, is to immediately seek to display his abilities in that area.

However, it is commendable that he sought to avoid bloodshed, even though he surely knew that his efforts would be for naught. We see that Jephthah's speech displayed himself as a man who knew Israel's history and God's Word when he spoke to the Ammonites. Some have criticized him for trying to negotiate with the enemies but then failing to show a similar grace to his brethren (12:2-4). This may be a justified criticism that points out the failures existing in all of us. He was right to seek peaceable means to resolve Israel's problem, but he was clearly wrong to react to the criticism of Ephraim. We will look at that more extensively when we get to that point of the story.

Jephthah's message to Ammon displays a number of interesting features. One is that he recounts the history of how Israel came to possess that land. What he says is accurate, and it dispelled any possibility that their possession was illegal. He attributes their victories to God, which is what we should always do. Then we notice that he identifies Ammon with the god Chemosh (11:24). Chemosh was the god of the Moabites, while Milcom was the god of the Ammonites (1 Kgs. 11:33; 2 Kgs. 23:13). This seems to indicate that Moab had become part of the Ammonite territory and that possibly Ammon had included the Moabite god as one of their own. Then we also note his statement in 11:26 concerning the 300 years that Israel had possessed the land. Jephthah's life can be dated to about 1078 B.C., so that with 300 years plus the 40 years of wilderness wandering, we arrive at an early date for the exodus from Egypt, about 1400 B.C. (Leon Wood, *Distressing Days of the Judges*).

Without closely examining the discussion he engaged in with Ammon, we can learn that knowledge of God's past dealings and the truth of His Word is a valuable tool to combat the foe. We can always test the claims of rationalism or worldly reasoning by the Word of God, and when we do this, it always reveals the emptiness of the claims made by natural men. The Lord commends the church in Philadelphia for having *"kept my word"* (Rev. 3:8), which seems to indicate that they knew His Word and guarded it as being valuable. Jephthah knew that Ammon had not been dispossessed by Israel; that had taken place prior to Israel's coming into the area and the Ammonites had lost their territory to the Amorites who were defeated by the children of Israel (Num. 21:21-25). In addition, Jephthah falls back, as we always should, on the claim that it was the LORD's work to give this land to Israel (11:23) and that He was the Judge whether their claims were right or not (11:27). He lays bare the fact that their claim was unjustified by the facts, but God's enemies never willingly submit to or acknowledge the truth of God's Word.

Without any details being given in the historical record, we learn of his great victory and the deliverance that he wrought by God's power (*"the Spirit of the Lord came upon Jephthah,"* 11:29). The Ammonites were subdued under his hand and he delivered Israel. Being empowered by God for this work, he accomplished it without any difficulty, or so the record appears. The lack of any recounting of events seems to indicate that the battle, or battles, were not prolonged or detailed, and that Ammon was defeated handily.

Jephthah's Vow

Zeal should always be accompanied by scriptural and spiritual intelligence, but it seems that Jephthah lacked these qualities when he vowed to the LORD. One has said that Jephthah's vow was not a genuine vow but rather was a bargain with the LORD (C. A. Coates). In this way, it was much like Jacob's promise to God at the end of Genesis 28. As a bargain with God, it was unnecessary, since the Spirit of Jehovah was upon him and he really did not need more than that to gain a victory. It seems to express an unspiritual condition in his soul. It is evident that we can promise much for God and zealous activities may take place without the confirmation of God's Word to guide. We always need to be instructed by and restrained by His Word in what we promise or in what issues from our mouths.

The question of what he actually did in relation to his daughter is one that will likely never be answered by what we might say. It seems that his promise in 11:30-31 leaves ample room to think that she was devoted to the LORD for the rest of her life. This is based on several arguments:

1. Jephthah was intelligent enough in God's Word to know that the LORD would never accept a human sacrifice from anyone. In addition, what priest of Israel would be willing to participate in this act? And if he were to sacrifice her privately, it would not have been a sacrifice to the LORD, but to a pagan god, since God never accepted such sacrifices. That kind of sacrifice was characteristic of pagan worship. How could those of the nation of Israel who would hear about it tolerate this kind of action? It seems impossible that this would actually take place.

2. Jephthah's words seem to exclude the possibility of offering a human sacrifice, even though the idea of one issuing out of the doors of his house would seem to preclude any animal to be sacrificed. He uses the word "and" which, according to many expositors, can be translated "or." So that he expressed, it seems, two options in his vow: one is that it would be devoted to Jehovah and the other is that it would be offered up for a burnt offering. If that which met him was suitable for a burnt offering and acceptable to the LORD, then it would be offered in that manner; if not, it was to be devoted to the LORD and its value, if unclean, would be given to Him.

3. If Jephthah's words only include the idea of a human sacrifice, then we can understand why he was so distraught when his daughter came out to meet him; it would involve

a very great personal cost! However, it is equally true that his concern would have been the same if he knew that she would be devoted to a celibate life with no prospect of a family or children. Having a family and bearing children was considered a very important and valuable function in the lives of an Israeli family. Either way, she (and he) would bear the burden of the fulfillment of his vow.

4. If Jephthah sacrificed his daughter as a burnt offering, then how could he be included in the heroes of the faith in Hebrews 11:32? Would it have been God's character to commend a man who had violated the principles of God's Word in such a serious manner?

5. If his daughter was to be sacrificed as some think, then why did she spend the last four months bewailing her virginity and not her short life? Why, also, did she spend that period with her companions and not with her sorrowing father? In addition, how could the daughters of Israel go to lament the daughter of Jephthah four times a year (11:40) if she had been sacrificed? How would Israeli opinion and priestly convictions permit such an action in her case? In addition, some translations render the expression, "to lament," as "to rehearse" or "to talk with" the daughter of Jephthah. This indicates that she was living, not dead.

6. The fulfillment of his vow in 11:39 is immediately followed by the statement that "she knew no man." This seems to indicate that the fulfillment of his vow was the devotion of her to a celibate life in service for the LORD, not a sacrifice on an altar.

Adam Clarke, in his commentary, includes a lengthy quotation by Dr. Hale on this question that exposits the question from many aspects with the conclusion that she was devoted to the LORD and not sacrificed as a burnt offering.

Whatever one might conclude about this case, it only emphasizes the seriousness of making any vow to the Lord. Whether vows are to be made by believers in our day is another question, but we do know that whatever one might promise to the Lord in any manner should be considered seriously in view of what it will cost. Rash promises are always unwise, but they are often made in a situation of great anxiety and with the desire that as a result of doing so, God will be required to respond as we request. Nothing can put God in a position of obligation other than fulfilling His own will and manifesting His own character. We learn from Ecclesiastes 5:1-7, that God expects one to fulfill promises that are made to Him and this is demonstrated in many ways in the Old Testament as well as the New.

One might just suggest that Jephthah's daughter is a picture in this case of our Lord Jesus in that she was absolutely submitted to her father's will. She made no resistance to his decision and as a result, there were those who remembered her and honoured her action perpetually. Her pure life was given in devotion to the LORD and as our blessed Lord, she was left without any natural generation but with those who were identified with her in memory.

Jephthah's Failures

One would rather pass over the sad history of Judges 12:1-7, which records the failure of Jephthah to reconcile his own brethren, but it is a part of the divine record and must be considered. It suggests that there are aspects of failure in our own lives and in that of men who have sought to be faithful to God in their day, but who have also failed in some critical points. It is sad that a man who could defeat the enemies of God's people could not show more grace to his brethren even though their actions were far from commendable. Gideon had his failures at the end, but he was a man who had learned that *"a soft answer turneth away wrath"* (Prov. 15:1), a lesson that surely we all should seek to learn.

Ephraim's Resentment

It seems evident without doubt that Ephraim was wrong. They seemed to be a kind of people who were sensitive to being slighted by any omission, always wanting a prominent place and recognition. They had responded in the same way to Gideon in Judges 8:1-3. However, Gideon was one who knew them better than Jephthah did, and he had the temperament to deal with and appease them. Brethren like this have not ceased to exist today, of course! There always will be those who resent anyone else accomplishing anything or gaining any victory without including or recognizing them as well.

These Ephraimites showed the same character as the Philistines when they threatened to burn Samson's father-in-law's house upon him with fire (Judg. 12:1 with 14:15). We need to be very careful that we do not imitate their threats by retaliating against our brethren who have done something for God but who have not included us in the honour, possibly unwittingly. It is also so easy for any one of us to be much like them, jealous against others who might have done something more than we have and who have gained some honour that we think we should share. Envy leads to contention and it causes divisions between brethren.

However we may see their attitude, we know that, though it is not an easy thing to conciliate such brethren, we all have a tendency to react and retaliate against them. Jephthah represents a man who was quick to respond to insults and slights. He had not forgotten what they had done to him in his earlier years, and he had failed to learn the lesson of problems that they had caused by refusing to give others a place (Judg. 11:1-2). His brethren had left him out of the inheritance, but instead of identifying with those of like experience, he acted much as his own natural brothers had acted toward him.

His reaction to their insulting behaviour caused him, first of all, to defend himself. He emphasizes in 12:2-3 what **He** had done. Notice the repeated expressions, "I," "my people," "me." They are found 11 times in 2 verses. He is essentially accusing the Ephraimites as if to say, "You were the cause of your being left out of the battle since you failed to come when I called you." This may have been true, though there is no record of it in chapter 11. However, his words betray an attitude of righteous indignation against them that, instead of removing the cause of the conflict, only increased the intensity of the animosity between them. His attitude of resentment carried over to his men, the Gileadites, who reacted against Ephraim because of the insults being hurled against them (12:4). The antagonism increased, instead of being abated, so that it led inevitably to the carnage of brethren against brethren in verses 5-6.

Conflict Resolution

Do we learn anything about the causes of and resolution of conflict between brethren from this story? Ephraim should have considered the incendiary nature of their words in the first place and Jephthah should have recognized the innate sensitivity of the Ephraimites as well. If some wisdom and grace had been exercised, 42,000 Israelites, their brethren, would have been living instead of lying dead on the banks of the Jordan. We should learn something about the dangerous nature of our words against brethren as we read this account so that we might express a different attitude toward those who are our own brethren today, albeit the fact that they may be difficult to accommodate.

Division Between Brethren

However, another point needs to be touched on and that is the ease with which brethren can be divided, often in the very place where they should be united. The Jordan was certainly a point of their unity, speaking of their common entry into the land as a united people under Joshua's leadership. Yet, it became a point of division and death.

The test of fellowship was an issue that involved the native manner of pronouncing one word that was linked with that river. "Shibboleth" and "Siboleth" both meant "a stream, or flood," so that they were both saying the same thing but with words that sounded different. It is not hard to see how often brethren can be divided on issues or principles that may not be as significant as one might think.

That is not to say that there are not principles that are essential, doctrines that are vital. However, one should be very careful lest we allow elements that represent our own views or perceptions of Scripture to be over-emphasized so that they become elements of division that are unwarranted. At times, we have to admit, we can allow our own application of God's Word to be so used that it becomes "the issue" that determines what we think of another believer.

For a simple example, there have been those who would condemn a brother for wearing a red tie to a meeting or for sisters who might wear certain kind of shoes. Or the question may have been one's view of certain issues concerning doctrine or practice. The list could go on almost indefinitely, but we understand that what we might believe about the application of certain truths may be held as a personal conviction and should not be applied to other brethren or sisters. When the Word of God is clear and we can teach the truth from it, then we must stand firmly on it, but do so *"speaking* [holding] *the truth in love"* (Eph. 4:15). If we could learn this principle from Romans 14 and other passages of the New Testament, it would be a great blessing to assembly fellowship.

There are matters that must be dealt with in an assembly, or other practices that would limit fellowship. However, there can be a form of legalism that is especially evident to any who might be looking on impartially and who wonder how these things could ever become such great issues. We may not always perfectly agree with other brethren in everything; however, we must seek to go on in harmony with them as far as possible and not cut them off like Jephthah did to those who were his brethren. If he had exercised more grace and wisdom and if they had displayed more humility, such a slaughter by brethren would have never taken place on the banks of the Jordan River.

Problems and differences of this nature have caused divisions and splits among the saints for years. The case of what is called "the Bethesda question" by many is only one example, but the principle upon which men like Mr. Darby and others acted, continued to the point of dividing and cutting off families and assemblies. Such an action is contrary to the Scripture, but it seems that we can fall into it so easily, especially when brethren are conscientiously concerned to uphold right principles. God says to us, *"Be of the same mind one toward another. Mind not high things, but condescend to men of low estate. Be not wise in your own conceits"* (Rom. 12:16), and *"If it be possible, as much as lieth in you, live peaceably with all men"* (Rom. 12:18).

Fellowship with the saints is a precious thing in God's sight and we must seek to maintain it as far as possible by the power of the Spirit of God. We read in Ephesians 4:2-3, *"With all lowliness and meekness, with all longsuffering, forbearing one another in love; Endeavoring to keep* [guard] *the unity of the Spirit in the bond of peace."* Again, Psalm 133 reminds us of the preciousness of unity among saints. May the Lord preserve us from being instrumental to cause divisions among God's people!

It seems instructive that we read Jephthah judged Israel only six years (12:7). Six is a number of man in his weakness, and a man such as he was would be a weak man to lead and judge God's people. Previous judges had maintained peaceful conditions among the people of God for much longer periods, but they were different men from Jephthah. One who cannot handle men any better than he did would not be capable of such a responsibility. May we learn these truths from the examples of those who have gone before and seek to be the better for it!

Evil Again! The Philistines

For the seventh time, we read that the children of Israel did evil in the sight of the Lord (13:1). Their evil resulted in the Lord delivering them into the hand of the Philistines. These people seem to be different from the other enemies that had oppressed Israel. We have noted that they had come, possibly by way of Egypt, by a different route than Israel took to enter the land. Their previous location and origin is difficult to determine, but they had been in the land for many years prior to the exodus.

We learn in Genesis 21:32 and 34 that Abraham went into the land of Abimelech, the land of the Philistines. We find the same situation existed in Isaac's excursion into the same area (Gen. 26:1, 8, 14-15). We learn in Genesis 10:13-14, that the Philistines were descended from a common ancestor with Egypt (Mizraim) and Jeremiah 47:4 tells us *"the Lord will spoil the Philistines, the remnant of the country of Caphtor."* Archeological evidence also links them with Caphtorian culture.

They came out of Egypt (see Ex. 13:17) into the land and had occupied the area along the coast, southwest of Israel. God had intended that Israel would take and occupy all the land of the Philistines, but they failed to do so until they seem to have dominated that area during the reign of David and Solomon (1 Chron. 18:1). However, there was war with the Philistines throughout the remainder of Israel's history in the land until the captivity in Babylon.

It seems that the Philistine domination was the other half of the Ammonite control that Jephthah countered. During the same time that Jephthah was battling the Ammonites, Samson began to harass the Philistines. Israel was between these two enemies, but God raised deliverers who fought against them to bring a measure of liberty to His people. According to the suggested timeline of Judges, the Philistines began to dominate Israel about the middle of Eli's priesthood. If that point was when his sons were carrying on their evil behaviour (1 Sam. 2:12-17, 22), one can see another reason why they experienced such opposition from this quarter.

Philistines Represent

We have noted that the Philistines were a people who had come out of Egypt, as Israel had. Their name means "wanderers," and these represent people who have possessed the land belonging to God's people, but without divine direction. They had not come by the same route or by means of the same delivering power. They had never been in bondage in Egypt, neither had they cried for deliverance. They were never guarded by the bloodstained door, nor had they passed through the Red Sea. All the experiences of Israel at Mt. Sinai, with what God had revealed to them of Himself, were missing in their experience. They had their gods that seemed to mix the truth of Jehovah with false deities to some extent.

Therefore, we see them as a people who represent religious profession, occupying a place that has never been provided for them by the work of Christ, taking ground that is not truly theirs to enjoy in the realm of spiritual profession. They compose the vast mass of "Christendom" comprised of church members, workers, religious do-gooders, who pretend a place as Christians, but without the spiritual evidence of the new birth, nor the revelation of God to their souls. We are surrounded by these people and they are the greatest opposers of the gospel and the truth of God. For some of them, their appearance is so close to genuine Christianity that they seem real, so that there is an attraction and a similarity that causes difficulty to discriminate and recognize who they truly are.

These Philistines are notable in Judges 13 in that they are the only foreign nation that dominated Israel without causing any concern on Israel's part. We are amazed that they had control over Israel (at least the southwest part) for the longest period of time (40 years) and Israel was seemingly content to remain under their oppressing force. They were so reluctant to disturb the "status quo" that they intended to deliver their saviour, Samson, into the hands of the Philistines (15:11-13). The implication is that there is something unique about Philistine bondage.

When God's people are cold at heart toward God and warm at heart toward self and the world, they would rather accept religious profession and accommodate themselves to it rather than oppose it. It goes under the pattern of religious compromise, of acceptance of all who claim the name of Christ. We see it in the attitude that would rather accept wrong conditions than to cause any problem or difficulty. It is an attitude of toleration, of "getting along," rather than standing for the truth of God's Word.

It is an indication of extreme spiritual departure and weakness when this condition exists. Many, who profess to be God's people today, a day of Laodicean conditions, are drifting back into the religious world, accommodating themselves to religious practices that profess to represent true Christianity, but which are in reality far astray from the truth. It takes spiritual courage and determination, true repentance and exercise, to resist these conditions and to continue in faithfulness for the honour of the Lord Jesus and the truth of His Word.

Paul warned Timothy in his closing letter about these conditions. He spoke of men loving pleasure rather than loving God, then he says that they have a *"form of godliness, but denying the power thereof"* (2 Tim. 3:4-5). The only thing that will enable a man of God to effectively oppose this condition is the infinite power of God's Word, inspired and applied so as to save and deliver the people of God (2 Tim. 3:16-18). We recognize those conditions in our day, and we must refuse to become complacent and never be satisfied to allow this enemy to oppose and bind the people of God.

We will notice that God was not satisfied for them to remain in that condition either; He raised up a deliverer, a most remarkable and strange man, a man named Samson.

11

Sixth Recovery Under Samson
Laodicea and People's Rights
Spiritual and Moral Depravity Ensue

We have noticed a steady decline in the spiritual and moral condition of the nation of Israel during our studies in Judges. It seems that this decline reached its extremity in the conditions under the last judge and as seen in the recorded events following. This was the last time that we read, "*And the children of Israel did evil **again** in the sight of the Lord.*" There seems to be some significance in this being the last time, and it makes us think of the days that it represents ecclesiastically in relation to the church age (2 Tim. 3:1-5; 1 Jn. 2:18).

Last Typical Period

We have come to the last period of Judges, and both it and Samson, the judge, are typical. This period represents the church period that the Lord reprimands as he speaks to Laodicea in Revelation 3:14-22. As C. A. Coates puts it, "Samson was the last judge; and he represents the last intervention of God in the deliverance of His people before the kingdom is publicly set up." We note that complacency is seen in the case of the people at this point. We remember that they had wept when reprimanded by the angel in Judges 2:4, but at this point in Judges 13, there is no recorded expression of any desire for liberation from the domination of the Philistines.

Even more striking, we see that, for the first time, they were willing to side with their oppressors, and deliver into their hands the one that God had raised for that purpose

(Judg. 15:13). These are very strange conditions in which a judge would have to serve, but at this point we are looking at a very strange judge! In Samson, we see a judge who was raised of God to deliver a people who were not concerned about deliverance, so that this was an act of God moving sovereignly on their behalf. We can see that God raised up a man with "extra-ordinary" capabilities for these very difficult conditions. In addition, we observe that Samson was a strange expression of spiritual, divine power mixed with terrible, carnal weakness, so that what he was **offically** under God's hand was a stark contrast to what he was **personally**.

What God Intended

However, the character of Samson's call only reflected what God had intended Israel to be; they, like him, had departed from that calling through their own failure and departure. It is noteworthy that for the most part, God raised men to lead His people who reflected the condition of the people in that day, so that they were an expression of Israel's own character.

This presents a lesson for those who might criticize leaders and elders among the saints in an assembly, and who would draw attention to their shortcomings and failures; normally, those men are only expressing what the assembly has been during the years of their development. In addition, those who criticize these men need to consider that they are the best that such an assembly has for that position of responsibility. It should also be pointed out that the very ones who criticize will very likely not be any better than those who presently are the objects of their criticism.

Unique Character of Samson

Samson is unique among the judges in that he was the only one with "superhuman" strength and ability. God, knowing the desperate condition of His people, marvelously raised a man who was powerfully equipped to overcome the domination of the Philistines so that Samson comes on the scene with the greatest potential to use for God. However, what is sad is that he was the weakest of all the judges in his personal character. Strength imparted by God was his, but his downfall was the weakness of the flesh. It emphasizes to us that spiritual power and ability to be used by God for a great work will not compensate for a lack of inward character and moral strength. God can use even failing, faulty, and feeble vessels to accomplish His work (1 Cor. 1:27-28); what is more important is what He would seek to produce in us that expresses conformity to His will. That work **in us** may be more difficult than what He is able to do **through us** toward others.

Samson is also unique among the judges in that he was the only one who was never helped by any of his nation. He never led an army against the enemy, not even 300 men as Gideon had! He accomplished all of his deeds without the fellowship of his brethren, and in some cases, in spite of them. More than that, his own brethren were willing to bind him to deliver him to the Philistines (15:13). His acting individually presents a typical picture of a Nazarite acting for God in last day conditions. In 2 Timothy, Paul addresses that young man, reminding him that he must maintain Nazarite conditions (spiritually) in his life and service for God (1:9, 13; 2:3-4, 21; 3:12, 17, etc.). The feature of the Nazarite that Timothy displayed was the principle of separation to the Lord.

As with Samson, Paul also reminds Timothy that he will need to stand for God alone, as Paul did in his latter days (1:15; 4:16). Second Timothy portrays the man of God standing steadfastly for God without the comfort or support of other believers with him. It reminds us that if one intends to serve God faithfully in last days, he must be prepared for opposition, even from misunderstanding or unspiritual brethren. The call to the overcomer in Laodicea addresses him as an individual who responds to the Lord's voice to enjoy communion with Him alone (Rev. 3:20).

Characteristics of Laodicea

In Samson and in the chapters that follow, we see characteristics that correspond to the condition of the Laodicean assembly in Revelation 3:14-22. We notice that Jephthah ended his public service by displaying a marked lack of "brotherly love," when he was responsible for slaying his brethren. Philadelphia (Rev. 3:7) means "love of the brethren," but in Laodicea, it is no longer "love of the brethren," but rather it is "love of self." We can see that the professing church has also displayed that change in affection and character that typifies the last days.

Samson was a man who was unfaithful to his calling and unresponsive to God's purposes for him; we notice that the Lord, when He speaks to Laodicea, tells them that He is the One who is *the Amen, the faithful and true witness*" (Rev. 3:14). He draws attention to their unfaithfulness and infidelity. They failed to measure up to the standard that He expressed in His character and service. God called the church to be a true and faithful witness to the Lord, but how it has failed!

The Lord says to Laodicea that His analysis of their works revealed that they were, shall we say, indifferent and careless. They displayed little exercise in their activities, with the result that He considered their works to be repugnant to Him. As we examine Samson, we will see that nothing that he did was done out of genuine love for God's people, neither out of any devotion to the Lord. He did everything without that lofty purpose; he did everything for Samson, for self-gratification, and not through submission to the will of God. It seemed as if Samson saw his conflict with the Philistines, not as a work to deliver Israel, but rather as a kind of personal contention, almost as a "game" to play, with these people. His failure lay in his close and personal involvement with those who were God's enemies. In him, we see a man who was unconscious that his own condition was so contrary to God.

In addition, he was unconscious of the dangers inherent in his involvement with Philistine women. He lost his source of power during a period of sleep (unconscious condition) while Delilah had a man shave the seven locks of his head. His sleeping on her lap seems to be typical of his spiritual condition, unconscious of his danger while dallying with the Philistines and unresponsive to the high calling that was his. Paul reminds the believers on more than one occasion that they needed to awake out of sleep (Rom. 13:11; Eph. 5:14). Sleeping, or being unaware of one's true state, is the Laodicean condition, (Rev. 3:17). The

Lord reproves that church for being unaware of their actual state and it seems clear that they had lost their power.

The power of God's people is always linked with separation to the Lord from every element that is contrary to Him. Samson never maintained the separation required by his Nazarite conditions. The same is true of Laodicea, unconcerned about upholding a standard that the Lord will accept. What Samson was, personally, introduced the conditions that followed in the remaining chapters of Judges. His failure to lead the people in victory over the Philistines and in spiritual recovery produced the spiritual evil and moral depravity that ensued. We see this pattern being duplicated when we look at the predicted conditions of the last days before the Lord's coming. Spiritual failure in Samson, who was the leader and deliverer, allowed further declension among the people, and this is what we would anticipate prior to the rapture of the church.

Self-Centered Life

Strangely enough, Samson was a man who, though moved four times by the Spirit of God, (13:25; 14:6, 19; 15:14), knew almost nothing of fellowship with God in his life. He prayed only twice in the record of his life, (Judg. 15:18; 16:28) and in both cases, his request was for the satisfaction of his own desires and never for God's honour or the blessing of God's people. Samson lived a life that was self-centered, self-indulgent and self-complacent, and the Lord exposes the same condition in Laodicea. This describes the state of Christian testimony in the last days before the Lord comes. These conditions are predicted in God's Word (2 Tim. 3:1-9; 4:1-4).

We realize, before we judge Samson too harshly, that his life typically expressed conditions that can very easily prevail in our own lives. We should ask ourselves if these conditions are not often our own. Do we manifest genuine commitment to the Lord and His service in our lives, or do we essentially live for ourselves? When we pray, is the essence of our prayer centered upon our own wants and wishes, or personal desires for what would please us? Or do our prayers reflect our experienced communion with the Lord, centering on real desires to fulfill

His will and to seek His blessing on the saints as well as those not saved? We think of a prayer that speaks to this:

> I often say my prayers, but do I really pray?
> Or do the wishes of my heart dictate the words I say?
> Far better to kneel down, to gods of wood and stone,
> Than offer to the Living God a prayer of words alone.
> —author unknown

Are we satisfied with ourselves, our condition of life, or our own abilities, sadly unaware of the conditions that exist to which the Lord would seek to call our attention? We should beware that we do not follow the same pattern as Samson did and thus fail to accomplish God's will in our lives! Self-complacency is a great enemy of God's people. It seems to be the prominent feature of those in Laodicea that was most obnoxious to the Lord. It produced satisfaction with their existing condition; it prevented any judgment of self or examination of themselves before God. It kept them from realizing their need of God and dependence on Him for everything. They were so complacent in their state that "need" was the last thing in their thoughts. We notice in Revelation 3:17 that they were complacently content with their own estimation of self, though the Lord saw something entirely different. That was Samson and that can be our condition also!

Our spiritual state can be detected by the character of our prayers. We can be very "light" in our praying, expressing very little of a deep burden of heart and only saying words, perhaps the same ones repetitiously from the past. May both Samson and Laodicea speak to us and produce some sense of our deep need of God and His power at work in our lives and in the assemblies of His people.

Samson's Parents and God's Promise

Samson's birth mercifully expressed God's sovereignty. There appears to be no exercise in the nation of Israel for deliverance, no cry to God, no concern, and neither was there any exercise by his mother to have a child (Judg. 13:1-3). It would seem that this was the only case of barrenness without concern in the Bible, for in all other occasions that Scripture records, barren women expressed a desire before God to have a child. We see this in the cases of Sarah, Rebecca, Rachel, Hannah, and Elizabeth. So that for a nation that was unconcerned about their servitude (no crying to God for deliverance), and from a mother who was unconcerned about her barrenness, God raised a man to be a saviour of His people.

In addition, Samson came from the tribe of Dan, the last tribe that one would likely have considered the channel that God would use. Only a few chapters farther (chapter 18), we read of a part of that tribe falling into gross idolatry early in their history, and Dan, in Scripture, never appears to be depicted in any attractive way.

However, God was determined to work to deliver His people and to defeat their enemy, and He chose to act in this way. It illustrates to us that God can and will work despite the unfitness and helplessness of His people, simply because it is His purpose to do so and because of His own mercy. This act didn't depend on their crying to God or their seeking deliverance. God delivered them for Himself, as He speaks in Isaiah 63:5: "*And I looked, and there was none to help; and I wondered that there was none to uphold: therefore mine own arm brought salvation unto me; and my fury, it upheld me.*" There seem to be times when God works in response to the cries of His people; there are other times when He will work solely because of His own sovereign purpose.

Toleration of Philistine Bondage

We have seen that this particular enemy, Philistine, was the only one that didn't seem particularly offensive or oppressive to Israel. This indicates that there was something unusual about Philistine bondage (spoken by Jack Hunter of Scotland in oral ministry at Bible Conference in Vancouver, B.C., Canada). The Philistines clearly represent something different from the seven wicked nations of the land that God commanded Israel to destroy and dispossess. While we have dealt with this in the previous chapter, it bears repeating since the Philistines represent an insidious enemy today. The Philistines had their origin and connection with

Egypt (Gen. 10:13-14), for we read that Mizraim (Egypt, see Gen. 50:11) begat Casluhim, and from him came Philistim. We see these connections also indicated in Jeremiah 47:4 and Amos 9:7.

So the Philistines came from Egypt into the land, but they never experienced Egyptian bondage, never knew deliverance by the blood applied in the Passover night, did not pass through the Red Sea or come by way of the journeys that Israel had taken. Their name means "wanderers," and they had come to that land without clear direction from God, they had wandered until they settled there. They had a form of worship that was similar to the true worship of Jehovah in many ways and they occupied a place in the land that made them as "thorns in the sides" of Israel constantly.

In this way, they represent those who occupy a place in Christendom and seek to dominate God's people so that Christian profession abounds and is accepted nearly everywhere. They would bind and limit the exercise of the liberties of God's people. They are the ones who proclaim that a man cannot preach the gospel, baptize, or teach believers unless he has been ordained. They deny believers the privilege of obeying the Lord in local assembly functions, including remembering Him in the breaking of bread, apart from their own system. Restrictions multiply, and sadly, many believers who once enjoyed the freedoms of the local assembly are willingly returning to the bondage of a clerical system.

Philistines are found where the emphasis is on what will attract the flesh, such as incense, vestments, stained glass and professional musicians to entertain. Philistines would never preach against anything unless it is contrary to their system; they arrange and express everything in order to make the people feel comfortable and satisfied in their present condition, never preaching about sin, judgment, repentance and conviction. The Philistines represent those who have a *"form of godliness, but deny the power thereof"* (2 Tim. 3:5). They are *"lovers of pleasures more than* [rather than] *lovers of God"* (3:4). Let us not assume that these are only found in the realm of Christian profession outside the sphere of assemblies; sadly, this is a condition that is also increasingly evident among some assemblies in these last days.

Manoah's Wife

It must have been a surprise to Manoah's wife to have the angel of the Lord appear to her. Of course, he appeared as a man (v. 6, 8), but in reality this was a preincarnate appearance of the Lord Jesus Himself, a Christophany. Not since Gideon, in Judges 6, had the angel of the Lord appeared to anyone. The time factor is not absolutely clear in Judges, but that appearance had likely been at least 100 years prior to this moment. So this event immediately indicates an act of divine intervention by which God was manifesting His mind. He would not leave His people under the control of an external power without moving to deliver them. We need to constantly affirm that **there is no religious system in Christendom that is God's will or is what the Bible teaches.** Repeatedly, in the history of the church, God has raised men to deliver His people and to overcome the power of established religion. In the case of this woman, and without any expressed desire on her part, He told her that she would have a son. Then He gave her the conditions that He expected her to maintain in her life prior to his birth. If she was going to have a Nazarite son, then she, as the mother, was required to maintain Nazarite character.

Israel had failed to remain separated unto God and had failed to maintain purity in its testimony. She and her son were to be what Israel had not been through the years. It teaches us that in a world of empty religious profession that displays departure and unfaithfulness, God desires and will use those who are a contrast to the prevailing condition. We never achieve power with God and with men through compromise and acceptance of a lower standard. That power depends on believers seeking to rise to the standard that God expects and through their displaying a life that is consistent with His purpose. This woman teaches us that if we desire to raise men and women for God in local assemblies, it requires that the older generation also seek to be the same.

The Nazarite Character

The characteristics of the Nazarite vow were physically displayed in three different areas of life. Those characteristics should be true in their spiritual application to the lives of believers today. For example, we would not expect a brother to allow his hair to grow; it would be contrary to the teaching of Paul in 1 Corinthians 11:14. But believers should display the spiritual characteristic that the Nazarite's uncut hair symbolized. The same is true regarding the abstinence from eating grapes or avoiding a dead body. What we see physically or materially displayed in the Old Testament has its counterpart in spiritual truth of the New Testament teaching.

The vow of a Nazarite is described in Numbers 6 but God mandated the conditions necessary for anyone who would desire it. The vow was voluntary, taken out of personal devotion to the Lord, but if he took that vow, the Nazarite had to maintain three essential conditions in his or her life. He must avoid contact with any form of the grape, from its kernel to the husk, including the wine produced from it. Thus, he typically separated himself from all that produces intoxication or excess of natural joys in one's life. In other words, he had to control his APPETITE. There are many aspects of the joys of this world and the flesh that can appeal to the child of God. These things will only stifle our expression of devotion to God if we indulge them. Many saints, who could be spiritual Nazarites, are hindering their spiritual exercise by their occupation with the amusements, entertainment, sports, literature and other elements of the world. This includes, in our day, the internet and the wide variety of things that one can see in it.

The Nazarite was marked by his APPEARANCE. He was not to cut his hair all the days of his vow. This was the outward expression of his testimony as a Nazarite. It was the crown of his vow ("separation" and "consecration" in Numbers 6 translate the same word as used for the crown of the high priest in Ex. 29:6, 30). The uncut hair also expresses subjection to the Lord's authority. It is worth noting that it is the same expression as Paul uses in 1 Corinthians 11:15 where he speaks of a woman wearing long hair (present active subjunctive verb). Allowing her hair to grow is the outward expression of her subjection to God's order, so it is a glory to her. In the case of both, the longer that they maintained that condition, the longer the hair would (normally) be if it were allowed to grow.

The last condition for the Nazarite was that he must avoid contact with a dead body of any person (Num. 6:6-9), including those who were near of kin. That signifies care in our ASSO-CIATIONS. Death is the result of sin working in the flesh, so it suggests those fleshly activities that would cause the loss of fellowship with God. They could be moral, or they could suggest the working of pride, self in any form, or other influences. The only way a Nazarite could avoid such contact was not to get too close to anything that would cause defilement. He must be careful in his involvement with the different influences and evil elements of his life in this world.

We notice that there are three men of our Bible who seem to be identified as Nazarites, if not totally by name, at least in their characteristics. Samson was the only one in Scripture personally called a Nazarite, but Samuel and John Baptist manifested at least some of those characteristics. Samuel's mother, Hannah, promised God that if she received a son, there *"shall no razor come upon his head"* (1 Sam. 1:11). The angel told Zachariah that his son *"shall drink neither wine nor strong drink"* (Luke 1:15). If all these were Nazarites in some way, we notice that theirs was a life-long condition. Any person could take a vow of the Nazarite for any period of time (Num. 6). These particular cases involve men that God raised up in very dark days of Israel's history. God needed men who would devote their entire lives in total service for Him. In addition, they were Nazarites, not through personal exercise, but by divine calling or by parental exercise.

Let us apply these truths to ourselves: God's desire for His people is that from the moment of their conversion, they will live entirely for Him in separation from the flesh and the world, expressing their devotion to Christ by their manner of living. How many of God's people have an exercise to rise to that divine calling? In addition, it should be the exercise of spiritual parents, or of older saints regarding younger believers, to raise the younger ones so that they will become useful for God in this capacity. Perhaps we do not raise spiritual "Nazarites" because of our own failure to manifest that character in our lives!

We see there were three requirements for Samson's mother

in order to raise a Nazarite in Judges 13. First, she must maintain Nazarite conditions personally. Second, there must be exercise to seek divine instruction in the home (13:12) so as to know how to raise the child, or what God's purposes were for him. In the third place, those parents displayed a desire to worship the Lord sacrificially (3:19). If these conditions characterized our homes, they would be places where the children would be raised for God, and His name would be honoured through them. More than that, if these are the conditions of a local assembly, we will see the younger ones take on the same characteristics.

Samson's Life and Descents

Samson's life and service commence at the end of chapter 13. His first movements under the Holy Spirit's control were in his home area. Other men often have pointed out that service for God begins in this way. It begins from the standpoint of our proving God and serving Him in our own home environment then moving out to a larger field. If a believer is not moved by (controlled by) the Holy Spirit in his immediate surroundings so that he is able to live and serve there, he will not do so elsewhere. This divine control indicates what God desired to exercise in Samson's life and service for God. In order to effectively serve God and deliver Israel, he needed to be submissive to God's will. This, as we will see, was one element that was lacking in his life and led to his failure. If a believer wants God to use him, he must be willing and exercised about submitting to God's will.

We see that Samson began on a high point but from then on, his life was a series of descents. He continually *"went down"* (14:1, 5, 7, 19; 15:8; 16:21). It is good to see that mingled with those goings down, he also *"went up"* (14:2, 19; 16:3, 31). It is not hard to see that our lives can be marked by "going down," but, thankfully, also by "going up." Life is not static in any sense, certainly not spiritually. If we are not going up, then we are surely going down. If an assembly is not progressing spiritually, then it is most certainly regressing. The only way to "go up" requires exercise and effort on our part. We either drift (going down) or we discipline ourselves unto godliness (1 Tim. 4:7-8; 6:11). We gladly note that Samson's last move (after his death), was to be *"brought up"* (16:31), and it reminds us that the last direction the saints of God will take is to be "brought up," regardless of the failures that have taken place.

Another general observation on Samson's life that we should notice is that he was constantly losing things that were very important. First, he lost his separation in chapter 14. Then he lost his purity in 16:1. His vital secret was lost in 16:17 and that resulted in his loss of power (16:20), liberty and sight (16:21), and finally, his life (16:30). Can we learn a lesson from his life? There are spiritual truths and essential secrets of the believer's life that we need to guard and treasure above all else. If believers prize those principles of Christian living that enable spiritual power, not allowing them to slip away, then a good measure of usefulness for God will ensue. What finally took place in his life was only the result of the steps he took at the beginning, since he never turned back or changed his course. Be careful what direction your life takes and where the little steps and actions are leading you! We need to make a good start in our Christian life, and then we need to continue in the same character.

Samson's Eyes

We cannot look at Samson's life in detail, but we learn from his experience that his greatest problem was his eyes. It was what he saw that caused him to respond as he did. We remember that it was Eve's sight of the tree and its fruit that caused her to disobey the Lord's command in the garden. We note that Lot made his decision based on what he saw in the well-watered plains of Jordan (Gen. 13:10). Achan committed sin and brought defeat to God's people by his attraction to what he saw (Josh. 7:21). We could multiply examples to illustrate this truth, but we should learn a lesson from these failures. What attracts our sight often will result in disobedience of God's Word and our going down in the spiritual life.

When Samson went down, failure usually resulted. When he went up, he was able to overcome. Does not that happen in our lives as well? Certainly! A child of God who occupies himself with those things that tend to attract his heart away from

God usually ends up going that direction in his life. Is that not the danger of allowing visual attractions from the entertainment world to have a place in our homes? If we allow a place for those devices that constantly present to us worldly attractions from Hollywood or Madison Avenue, they inevitably will become our occupation and affect our spiritual state. Many a child of God has gone down spiritually by bringing the television or videos into his home, even though at the outset he denied that it would affect his spiritual state. We become used to the things that we look at with desire or interest and they become the objects of our heart's pursuit.

Philistine Women in Samson's Life

We also see an important feature of Samson's life, and that is that his problem centered around three women, and all of them had a bad influence on him. They represent attracting influences of the world that seek to captivate the heart of a believer. While the Lord used the first one to seek *"an occasion against the Philistines"* (14:4), it certainly was not God's will for him to become thus involved. God worked behind the scenes, using his personal attraction to the woman in this chapter to cause Samson to fight the Philistines. Is it not ironic that Samson never seemed to see the Philistines as God's enemies? It was only as they harmed him that he fought with them. He was constantly dallying with Philistines, but Philistine men eventually put out the eyes that Philistine women attracted. He began with an attraction to a Philistine woman and ended his liberty and power on the lap of another.

Dear child of God, do we fail to recognize spiritual enemies for what they truly are? Is it possible that God's people, called to live holy, separate lives, are dabbling with elements that are only an essential part of the devil's program to cause their downfall? Philistines might represent an aspect of spiritual temptation that does not appear to be as evil as others are. Many believers who would avoid the grossly immoral aspects of temptation in their lives willingly occupy themselves with things that are not quite as offensive. There are believers who spend hours watching certain programs on the television or going to "family oriented" entertainment. What are these, but different means that the devil has to attract the flesh and rob God of the place He should have in our lives?

Even more, we see that Samson's attraction to these women also warns us of the danger of personal, emotional involvement with unsaved partners in life. Many lives that God could have used, lives that had potential and ability, have been lost and ruined through wrong relationships resulting in an unequal yoke. Be careful to guard your emotions! A beautiful (or handsome) form and an appealing personality may be the means that the devil will use to ruin your life for God.

The Woman at Timnath

The first woman (14:1) represents natural influences that, in themselves, do not appear offensive. She was likely attractive, for *"she pleaseth me well,"* Samson said (14:3, 7). His attraction to her was entirely on a physical, emotional level. He was manifesting the characteristic of Israel in the end of this book: *"every man did that which was right in his own eyes"* (21:25). Self-will demands its satisfaction, and in doing so, Samson also forced his parents to do something that was contrary to their convictions. He not only went down himself, but he brought his mother and father down with him. Self-pleasing never affects the individual only; it will draw others as well, causing them to do things that their conscience forbids them to do.

In order to go to where she was, Samson had to pass through vineyards, a place a Nazarite should never have been. We never find that he ever drank wine or ate grapes, but he was near the forbidden object. While there, he contacted the dead body of a lion that he had killed previously (14:5, 8-9). The Nazarite vow never forbad him to contact the dead body of an animal, but again, he was coming close to the forbidden. It could be possible that believers, who would never actually do anything contrary to God's Word or to do something expressly forbidden, yet would come as near as they can to it. In both these aspects, he was already nearly violating the conditions of his divine calling. It teaches us that, in order to satisfy our personal desires that are contrary to God's will, we will usually be found doing or in contact with elements that are contrary to our high calling (Eph. 4:1-2). Spiritual failure always involves compromise in divine standards.

Then Samson, at the wedding feast, finds himself in wrong company, with thirty Philistine companions to while away the time. Perhaps these companions were given that they might guard him, due to his known strength, from doing something harmful. They were expected to control the man who God intended would deliver Israel from their power. During that week, his prospective, unfaithful wife learns and discloses his riddle to the companions. Do we not learn from this that the Philistine element will always seek to control those who God would desire to use in order to bring about their defeat? In order to do this, they seek to learn and betray the secrets of God's people to use them to defeat the believer. Be careful, child of God, about becoming too close to the unsaved, even though they might appear attractive to your heart. Many believers have found that they have given up the secret of their spiritual power and they have suffered loss because of it.

Samson was disappointed in this first relationship, for when he returned to take her as his wife, he learned that her father had given her to his companion (15:1-2). He learned very soon that the Philistines are not those to depend upon. They easily violated promises and proved to be treacherous in their dealings. They were only acting as men of the flesh, but God was seeking to use their trickery to cause Samson to treat them as his enemy, not his friends. He retaliated by using the unclean jackals (foxes) with the firebrands to burn their standing corn. He, at this point, did not hesitate to stoop to employ an unclean animal to accomplish his vindictive purposes.

Following his retributive act upon the Philistines, Samson went down and dwelt in the top of the rock Etam (15:8). It was evidently a wild place with a name that signified, "place of ravenous beasts." However, he was safer among such beasts, which would not harm him, than among the Philistines with their treachery. Better to dwell alone, on the top of the rock, in dependence upon and in fellowship with God than to mingle with the uncircumcised Philistines. However, they were not satisfied to leave him alone in that place, but they came down to seek to take him (15:9-10). Their desire was to gain vengeance for what he had done to them. It was thus all of Samson's life; "tit for tat," no determined purpose for his actions, but only his desiring to wreak havoc for what they had done, followed by their subsequent retaliation. How often this seems to be the pattern of believers' lives. No determination, no submission to God's will, no direction nor purpose in their lives, with the result that they have accomplished nothing for God at the end of their days.

Samson would not use his power against his own brethren, but he did allow them to bind him and deliver him to the hands of the Philistines (15:11-13). His submission to the men of Judah did not hinder his power, for he broke the two new ropes and slew the Philistines when he came to them (15:14-15). It was a sad day when the men of Judah willingly bound God's servant to deliver him to the Philistines. It suggests (as F. C. Jennings has written) the imposition of man-made rules upon God's people that serve to hinder the exercise of their freedom and service for God. There is some new rule, some requirement imposed, some determination made by some "council" that seeks to prevent obedience to God's command. However, in such cases as with Samson, the power of the Spirit of the Lord enables one to overcome and defeat such a foe with a great victory. In so doing, Samson used a strange weapon that his enemies would never have considered, a new jawbone from an ass. It might have been despised and thought of as nothing, but it signifies that if God is in it, a little thing can be used to bring about the deliverance of His servant.

The Gaza Harlot

The second woman in Samson's life was a harlot in Gaza (16:1-3). She represents purely carnal, fleshly influences. Samson was interested solely in gratification of physical desires. Again, we notice that the Philistines sought to use lustful acts and enticements to bring about his defeat by shutting him inside the city. An act of this nature will always result in curtailment of the true spiritual liberty of a child of God and even cause total defeat. The enemy of our souls will seek to captivate the believer if he or she yields to the lust of the flesh and seeks to satisfy carnal desires. One lesson we can learn from his escape is that the believer has the power within him, given by God, to escape temptation of this nature (1 Cor. 10:13). This involvement, like all the rest in Samson's life, was simply the result of his exercising his own will in a wrong way; he was not seeking to do God's will, but rather, he was satisfying his own desires. Our wills, unless subjected to God's will entirely, will constantly lead us in a direction that will result in our spiritual downfall.

Delilah of Sorek Valley

The last woman, Delilah in the valley of Sorek, seems to represent a Satanic influence in our lives. She was possibly not a Philistine, but she had Philistine connections. She was a border-dweller, living between Israel and the Philistines. Samson could have thought, "What's wrong with her? She isn't the same as the other women that I have been involved with." He failed, as often we do, to discern the entangling element that she represented and how this apparently innocuous woman would be the cause of his ultimate downfall. Is that not the case with many believers? They ask, concerning some desired activity or relationship, "What's wrong with it?" rather than seeking to know if it is the Lord's will for them. "What is right about it?" and "Will this be a benefit to my spiritual life and testimony?" These should be our questions.

We find Samson playing a game with her, but the prize to be lost was his liberty, his sight, his power and eventually, his life. How foolish he was! How strange that his overwhelming love for this evil woman would overcome any ability to discern his danger in her lap! Does he not picture to us something that happens all too often? We think of a child of God, entangled in a relationship with a person or an activity, playing a game without realizing that it is effectively working to ruin his life and testimony. Little by little his resistance is broken down. Slowly she works and his answers get closer to the secret of his strength. F. C. Jennings shows how he comes closer and closer to the secret of his strength in his responses. Samson uses the number seven in his first response (*"seven green withs,"* 16:7). Then his second response pertains to ropes that *"never were occupied,"* or untouched (16:11). Then he came to the *"seven locks of my head"* in 16:13. Finally, he told her all his heart (16:17) and she learned the secret, and then the end came.

Defeated on Her Lap!

Sadly, like many in a similar condition, he assumed that he could go on as before despite losing the symbol of his separation and the secret of his power. However *"he wist not that the Lord was departed from him"* (16:20). So gradually had he come to that point that he did not realize that he had crossed the line and lost all that was precious and important. Head shaved, hair all gone, eyes put out, and liberty lost, we see Samson grinding in the Philistine prison. It was necessary that he lose his power when he lost his hair. He had already been careless about the other terms of his Nazariteship by passing through the vineyard and by contacting the dead bodies, though not actually violating those terms. Only one aspect remained, his hair. That hair represented the last and essential element of his calling, the outward testimony of what he was to be. It was the crown of his position before God, but now, having failed so miserably, he must lose this last vestige of that place and with it, he lost everything.

Does not this appeal to us as well? How many terms of your Christian character, dear child of God, have you violated in your life? Is it not possible that we might go on for years, having failed to exercise self-judgment in the sight of God, but still possessing sufficient strength that we can continue outwardly? Finally the last step is taken, and the results are, though possibly unexpected, only the end of all that has gone before. Far better if we could recognize the danger of the first step, that initial tendency toward world-entanglement, and draw back, seeking renewed fellowship with the Lord through repentance and forsaking that sin.

Samson's eyes were his trouble, and finally God's judicial dealings with him resulted in his eyes being put out. Others have noted that the last of the judges was blind; the last of the kings of Judah was blind; and the last of the seven churches in Revelation 3 is blind. What a terrible end for those who have been enlightened and have known the truth! In Samson's case, God removed the source of his problem. It may have been a mercy, but it occurred at the point of his life when he was near the end. John tells us about the danger of the lust of the eyes (1 Jn. 2:15-17), and there is an abundance in this world that has the potential to attract our eye. This is the point where Satan tries to allure the souls of God's people, and it is the one member that needs to be controlled by God's Word. Be careful what you look at with desire! It may be the element that will bring about your downfall and ruin your life for God.

Samson's End

Knowing the story well, we only need to note that Samson, who had killed many Philistines in his lifetime, slew far more at his death (16:30). It is not difficult to see a spiritual lesson in this event, that death to self wins the greatest victory for a child of God. That old problem that Samson failed to overcome in his life, the problem of self that assails us continually, was finally brought to an end.

However, it is touching to notice that God never totally abandoned His unfaithful servant. He is always like that! *"God is faithful,"* we read in 1 Corinthians 1:9, and that in view of the unfaithfulness of His own people. The Lord reminds those in Laodicea that He was the *"faithful and true witness"* (Rev. 3:14). He was faithful to Himself and His character (2 Tim. 2:13), and true in relation to God's testimony to them. He would disclose their true character so that they might judge that condition and receive Him for individual fellowship (3:20). Our response to His Word and His rebuke will always result in opening the door for Him to enter and for us to enjoy His communion.

Perhaps Samson knew God's presence personally for the first time in the prison. Whether true or not, as his hair grew again, he was gaining strength through divine enablement in view of his ultimate victory. Likely, the Philistines thought that with his hair once cut off, there was no hope for him to recover his strength again. They do not seem to have taken note that his hair grew in the prison. However, there is always hope of recovery for any child of God, no matter how far away one might be. In his solitary condition, alone with God, there can be restoration in the midst of sorrow. Samson's greatest victory came at the close of his life, and his defeat of the Philistines likely was instrumental in weakening them in view of greater victories by others who followed him.

May we learn from the life of this most powerful, yet weak, judge in Israel, something that will preserve us in the last days of Christian testimony so that we might be faithful and true to the Lord Jesus Christ until that moment when He appears to take us unto Himself.

12

"Right in His Own Eyes"
Spiritual Departure

The writer of Judges has not placed the last five chapters chronologically, since other references indicate that they occurred much earlier in Israel's history. The events of Judges 17-18 possibly took place during the days of Joshua or soon after, if we link Joshua 19:47 and Judges 1:34 with Judges 18:7, 28-29. In addition, Judges 20:28 indicates that the events of the last three chapters took place earlier, since Phinehas, the son of Eleazar, the son of Aaron was yet functioning. He would not have been serving if that chapter described events at the close of Judges, assuming that the period of Judges covers 450 years (Acts 13:20). He began his official duties as high priest at the close of the book of Joshua (Josh. 24:33).

We can conclude, then, that the Spirit of God has given us an "appendix" to the events of this book and has placed these chapters here for a different purpose. Since we are looking at the book, in part, as an allegorical presentation of the history of the church period, we suggest that their placement indicates that this departure is characteristic of conditions in the "last days." They would teach us those characteristics that we would expect to see in the end of those last days, or the conditions at the end of the church period.

The repeated phrase, *"there was no king in Israel"* (17:6; 18:1; 19:1; 21:25) means more than that those were days prior to the kingdom. It **does** mean that, of course, for these were the days of the judges. It means, typically, that these represent days before the Lord comes to set up His kingdom on earth and to rule over all. Being linked with the expression found twice, *"every* *man did that which was right in his own eyes"* (17:6; 21:25) it tells us that these days are connected with Laodicean conditions, when men reject the Lord's authority and His rule both personally and in the church. When writing to the assembly in Laodicea, the Lord exposes their attitude toward themselves and toward Him and His authority. They seemed not to need His presence and they rejected His position among them. Being satisfied with their condition, they were also self-directed and determined to plot their own course of activities without seeking to know His will. Sadly, this has been seen in a multitude of cases among those who profess to uphold the authority of Christ and to represent Him on the earth by their testimony.

When men ignore the Lord's authority, it is inevitable that every man will do that which is right in his own eyes. It means that men simply do what they think is right according to their own estimation, without seeking to know God's mind for them. However, the fact that there was no king in Israel never meant that they could or should do what they thought was right. Was not the Lord "king" in Israel? God intended Israel to be a theocracy. Did not Gideon remind them that the LORD would rule over them (8:23)? If they had sought to know His will, He would have directed them and preserved them from this terrible apostasy and sinful behaviour!

Sin of Israel Duplicated

The practices in these five chapters duplicated the sin of Israel at Mt. Sinai in Exodus 32:1-6. There, Israel had taken their eyes off the Lord and had fixed them on a man, Moses. He was absent from their presence for 39 days, (24:18) so they gathered around Aaron and demanded that he make them gods. Notice that they said, *"As for this Moses, **the man** that brought us up ... we wot not what is become of him"* (Ex. 32:1). In their minds, there was no king in Israel, so they did that which was right in their own eyes. Is not that characteristic of the last days? Is it not normal for men to get their eyes fixed on some great man and to ignore the Lord? Notice that what Israel did took place only one day short of Moses' return. His going up into the mount and having charged them to be obedient in his absence (24:14), pictures the present day when our risen Lord is absent, since He has gone back to the Father in heaven. How sad that it was only one day short of his return when they rebelled against the Lord! We are likely in the last days prior to the coming of the Lord Jesus. Let us seek to remain faithful for one more day, until He comes again!

The actions of Israel at Mt. Sinai followed the same order as those of Judges 17-21. First, they committed spiritual evil; they demanded that Aaron make them gods, so he made the golden calf. They had seen this form of worship in Egypt prior to their deliverance and were duplicating it. Following that deed of idolatry, they degenerated further and committed moral sin (Ex. 32:6, 18-19, 25; 1 Cor. 10:7). God gave the law on two tablets on which He wrote the Ten Commandments. Those commandments divide into two; the first four deal with God's rights and the last six treat man's rights. The action of Israel in Exodus 32 and again in these last five chapters violated both parts of the law. There is a principle that we can learn from God's Word, and it is that rejection of divine authority always results in moral degeneration. When God does not get His rights from men, neither will his fellow man receive his due.

Rejection of Christ's Authority

Man cannot uphold moral standards without right knowledge of God and recognition of His authority. We see this clearly taught in Romans 1. Man, knowing God in the beginning but rejecting that knowledge (1:21), commenced a degenerating slide that does not end until the final verses of the chapter that describe the resulting conditions of mankind. The conditions of the last days that Paul describes in 2 Timothy 3:1-9 are only the result of religious man's rejection of the truth of God (3:8). We should not be surprised by the increasingly degenerate conditions of our society, even of "religious men" and professing churches; those conditions are only the result of their having rejected the knowledge of God and His authority over them in the past. Permissiveness in practices, even to the extent of allowing homosexuals into "church fellowship," or "ordaining" them as preachers, is only one result of their having rejected the absolute authority of God and the binding directives of His Word.

There is a statement by A. W. Tozer in a very interesting and provocative article called, "The Waning Authority of Christ in the Churches," in which he states, (and it is worth quoting extensively):

> "Let me state the cause of my burden. It is this: Jesus Christ has today almost no authority at all among the groups that call themselves by His name. By these I mean not the Roman Catholics nor the liberals, nor the various quasi-Christian cults. I do mean Protestant churches generally, and I include those that protest the loudest that they are in spiritual descent from our Lord and His apostles, namely, the evangelicals.

> "The present position of Christ in the gospel churches may be likened to that of a king in a limited, constitutional monarchy. The king…is in such a country no more than a traditional rallying point, a pleasant symbol of unity and loyalty much like a flag or a national anthem. He is lauded, feted and supported, but his real authority is small. Nominally he is head over all, but in every crisis someone else makes the decisions…

> "Among the gospel churches Christ is now in fact little more than a beloved symbol…Not only does Christ have little or no authority; His influence also is becoming less and less. I would not say that He has none, only that it is small and diminishing. . . What church board consults our Lord's words to decide matters under discussion? Let anyone reading this who has had experience on a church board try to recall the times or time when any board member read from the Scriptures to make a point, or when any chairman suggested that the brethren should see what instructions the Lord had for them on a particular question. Board meetings are habitually opened with a formal prayer or "a season of prayer;" after that the Head of the Church is respectfully silent while the real rulers take over. Let anyone who denies this bring forth evidence to refute it. I for one will be glad to hear it."

The entire booklet is worth reading and presents an accurate critique of the condition that exists among the majority of "churches" today.

Micah and His Idolatrous House

The events of these last five chapters of Judges are linked in a number of ways. They are all associated with activities in the area of Mt. Ephraim, or the hill country of Ephraim and they both involve Levites (17:1, 7; 19:1). The first event involved breaking the first table of the law and the second event broke the second table of the law. Every one of these sordid actions touched negatively on the name of God or the Law of God, as does every evil act that men express.

We find Micah and his mother living in Mt. Ephraim at the opening of this story. We note, first, that his location in Mt. Ephraim was near where Joshua had lived and where he was buried (Josh. 24:30) and where Eleazar, the high priest of Israel, was buried (Josh. 24:33). In addition, it was not far from Shiloh, where the tabernacle was located at that time (Josh. 18:1; 1 Sam. 1:3; Judg. 18:31). This feature places these events in a more serious light. This did not take place among those who were at great distance from the house of God nor was it due to the lack of any link with an illustrious, spiritual past. Apostasy and departure can take place even in those who are linked with blessed and precious memories as well as in those who may be near the place of God's truth. It illustrates the truth expounded in Romans 1:21-23, *"Because that when they knew God, they glorified him not as God, neither were thankful, but became vain in their imaginations and their foolish heart was darkened … and changed the glory of the incorruptible God into an image made like to corruptible man …"* The sin of Aaron in Exodus 32 took place in the shadow of Mt. Sinai, near the place where God was speaking to Moses.

Possibly this chapter occurred during the time when Israel was already practicing Baal worship, at least to some extent, at this early stage of their history. If this is true, then Micah and his mother likely thought that their images, ephod and teraphim were not so serious a form of departure and could have justified them. His mother's intentions were good (17:3), but the entire matter was contrary to God's Word. Intentions are not the most important criterion for judging any action!

The entire beginning of this matter reeks of sin and compromise. Micah had stolen the silver from his mother and only confessed his sin after she pronounced a curse on the one who had stolen it. Then, after he confessed, she blessed him without any recorded rebuke. What kind of environment is this out of which to start a religious practice? It is much like what has marked Christendom in its practices: deceit, toleration, acceptance of any behaviour for the sake of peace and prosperity. Bad beginnings will always result in bad endings!

Justification of Wrong

One could imagine how the religious objects that he possessed could be justified. The images? Was there not a precedent for them since Aaron, the high priest, had made one at Mt. Sinai? An ephod? It was a garment of the priest, and Gideon had made one in his latter days (8:27). Teraphim? These were household gods, relatively innocuous and of long-standing practice. Had not Rachel stolen the teraphim from her father's house in Genesis 31:19? Possibly almost every person in Israel had them in their homes.

Those same justifications are brought out to argue for many wrong practices today. Someone of high standing has done this in the past, or "this is an object that will enable us to worship God better." It may be, "our denomination (or our group) has done it this way for a long time." Since these things have been done in this way for many years, they are assumed to be right. But they are not! If any practice is not according to God's Word, it is only another example of *"every man did that which was right in his own eyes."*

Jehovah's Name Linked with Idolatry

One of the worst aspects of this action, as well as that of Aaron in Exodus 32, was that it joined the name of Jehovah with an idolatrous system. Aaron proclaimed that these were Israel's gods that brought them out of the land of Egypt (instead of

ascribing that honour to the LORD) and then he made the proc-
lamation that the next day was a feast unto the LORD. That was
blasphemy, to link the LORD's name with an idol. The case in
Judges 17 is the same; his mother had dedicated the silver *unto
the LORD*" to make the images from and in the end of the chapter, Micah expected that the LORD would do him good with
a Levite for a priest. It is a practice often repeated for men to
link the name of the Lord with what they are doing out of self-
will. They make their own rules, determine their own practices,
erect their own idols, and then call the entire thing by the Lord's
name and drag that blessed name into association with what is
essentially evil. Sadly, like Micah, this is an evil that most fail to
recognize.

Micah put these religious icons in a house, consecrated his
son to be a priest (note that Jeroboam made two houses of gods
and consecrated anyone as his priests, even the lowest of the
people in 1 Kings 12:3. Wrong practices seem to persist for a
long time). Therefore, Micah had a man-made house of worship
and a man-made priest to officiate. However, "better things"
were yet to come.

The Levite-Priest seeking a Place

A Levite from Bethlehem-Judah came that way. Why was
a Levite from that city? It was not a Levitical city. There were
certain cities that had been set apart to be the Levites' possessions, but this was not one of them. It seems to indicate that
he was already wandering from the place that God intended
him to occupy, and subsequently, he went further in his quest
for a place. He was a man seeking a "better call," climbing to
a higher position. Micah contracted with him to perform his
religious services for a set fee, and all were content with the arrangement. Does it not seem strange that a Levite, knowing the
law of God and already having a work to do in God's House,
would so willingly agree with Micah to become something
that God never intended him to be? His action indicates that
mere knowledge never preserves anyone from doing wrong. A
deeper commitment to the Lord and His truth is essential. Yet
Micah was satisfied. He expected God's blessing, now that he

had a Levite as his priest (17:13). Do we hear echoes of that in our world today? "Get the right man, hire him to fill the job, and we are sure that God will bless us. We will see increase in numbers, great revival, and all will go well," even though it is contrary to God's order for His people. Be careful, brethren and sisters, that we do not accept those conditions as "normal."

No Outrage in Israel

It is worth interjecting an observation at this point. Do we notice that this kind of activity did not fill the tribes of Israel with indignation? However, in Judges 19-21, they reacted so strongly to moral evil that they almost destroyed an entire tribe from among Israel. It reminds us of the "under" judgment in 1 Corinthians 5:2 and the "over" judgment in 2 Corinthians 2:6-7. To this sin Israel never responded; in that sin they over-reacted! Why? There may be a few reasons involved:

1. It could be that Israel in general did not know what Micah was doing as well as what the men of Gibeah did.
2. They were all guilty of this sin to some extent, and therefore they could not judge their brethren for something that they were also doing. When men are doing wrong, it ties their hands when it comes to dealing with it in others.
3. They did not recognize this as the more serious sin. It is normal to consider moral sin more serious than a spiritual sin that infringes on God's rights. We should see spiritual evil as the cause of the following act and should deal with it as God requires.
4. It is easier to judge moral sin than spiritual evil. In the case of moral sin, there is a specific deed to act upon, whereas in spiritual departure, it is more difficult to identify the problem and respond appropriately. Only a spiritual person can do this and it must be done with wisdom and in the fear of God.

This seems to be a constant pattern in church history, and it can exist even among saints in assemblies. It is normal to tolerate the introduction of practices that may not be completely consistent with the Word of God; but the same persons who permit those practices will react swiftly and severely to judge any kind of moral misbehaviour. May we learn that what begins in a spiritual way will also be seen in moral actions eventually.

The Tribe of Dan Seeking a Place

Chapter 18 opens with Dan seeking an inheritance where they could dwell. This would not have been wrong, had it not resulted from their failure to drive the Philistines out of their possessions that Joshua had allotted to them. In addition, we read, *"the Amorites forced the children of Dan into the mountain; for they would not suffer them to come down to the valley"* (Judg. 1:34). They had sufficient territory given to them; to say that they did not is to say that the Lord had not given them enough land. He had known their needs and had given the land, but in their weak state, the Philistines possessed a good part of it. Not being able to drive them out (because of their unbelief), they were seeking an easy place to conquer and possess.

We can see this limited possession in the spiritual realm as we apply this to the church age. It was true of the believers who lived in Corinth. Carnal reasoning (Amorites) had forced them into an unproductive area of life and testimony that resulted in severe spiritual loss. It has been true even to our day. The church, instead of enjoying all that Christ has provided as a spiritual inheritance in the heavenlies (Eph. 1), has allowed the false reasoning of the world to dominate and direct its course so that actual practice has been on a lower level than God intended.

The failure to possess and be satisfied with all that has been given to us in Christ as our inheritance is often the cause of much restless activity among God's people today. Many *"run to and fro"* because they have no settled place where they can say with assurance that the Lord gave it to them and brought them into it.

A passing comment on Dan's condition is that believers often seek to take an easier pathway of life. The result is that they fail to move forward with confidence in God to enjoy all that He intends for them. Seeking an easier path with less difficulty has resulted in many believers falling into practices that are contrary to God's Word, even leaving an assembly for an easier place with fewer responsibilities. As with Dan, when a believer leaves the place where God has placed them, they usually end up much farther away than they anticipated. This tribe was searching for a place without seeking the mind of God in the decision, and this exposed them to the snare of the devil as they passed Micah's house. Faithfulness in the Christian life will always result in conflict with enemies and encounters against obstacles and opposition; however, it is the safest pathway, and by staying where God wants us to be, we will be preserved from those things that will result in ruin to our lives and testimony.

Encounter with the Levite

Evidently the band of Danites knew the Levite in Micah's house from previous encounters. It makes one wonder just where this young man had been! Hearing his voice made them stop to speak to him, and they asked him three questions. Those questions had to do with who brought him, what he was making (or doing), and what did he have there (Judg. 18:3). His unabashed answer was that it was himself and Micah all the way, and God had never brought him to that place. Man brought him there, he was working for a man, and he received his wages from a man. What a comedown for a Levite!

Not desiring to be overly severe, can we not see that these questions apply to anyone who accepts a place or position that is man-determined in a "church"? Isn't it the normal practice in Christendom for a man to agree to undertake a work and to do so much for so much pay. We don't want to be derogatory, for we know that there are many conscientious and dedicated men who are in such positions. It is the system more than them that is wrong, and nothing about it can be justified from God's Word. To be hired by men usually limits and hinders the ability of a man to speak the entire truth to the congregation. It is all too common for those who seek to do so, to find themselves terminated and sent on their way. Brethren and sisters, let us stay far away from anything that is even similar to this practice!

Three Important Questions

We could ask ourselves those three questions with regard to our fellowship in any activity or place where we might be found, including the local assembly. Who brought us to that place? If we are away from God and away from the assembly, who caused it? Some might say that God led them to leave, but it is hard to understand how God would lead anyone contrary to His Word! If we are in a local assembly, do we appreciate **who** it was that brought us there? Are we only there because of our family, or because our friends are there? Far better to be able to answer honestly, "It was the Lord who brought me here and I am here because of His presence."

Then, what are we doing there? An honest answer might be, that we are only coming and going, enjoying the fellowship and receiving spiritual food. But are we contributing? Are we a help to the work? Do we have any exercise about our responsibilities? We all have a part in an assembly fellowship, and if we all do our part according to the Scripture, wouldn't the assembly be a better place that would honour the Lord?

The last question is, "What do you have here?" The Levite had a house of gods, images, ephod, etc., but at least he knew what he had and what he was receiving from Micah for being there. But, what do we have when we are in assembly fellowship? Do we ever consider what we have received by the grace of God and what we have been brought to enjoy by our being there? Surely, words cannot express what has come our way by being a part of an assembly. These blessings come by way of appreciating the work of God in our lives and by establishing convictions that are settled on God's Word. Knowing these truths personally will always change our attitude and will encourage our full participation in the place where the Lord has brought us to be with Him.

The Danites confided in the Levite and asked counsel of him. Of course, he knew what they wanted to hear, so he gave them a smooth answer that they could apply in almost any way they desired. So on they went, and they found that, amazingly, the Levites' words were true. They found a people at ease, undefended, easy to be overcome and with a land that indicated prosperity. The fact that it was far from God's house, and far from the people of God seemed to be unimportant. They saw the potential for prosperity, so they followed in the steps of poor Lot as he moved into the well-watered plains of Jordan and pitched his tent toward Sodom (Gen. 13:10). What they saw, no doubt, gave them the assurance that it was of the Lord to pursue that course. That may have seemed right to those who were *"doing what was right in their own eyes,"* but to *"walk by sight"* (2 Cor. 5:7) is always a dangerous course. They never practiced what James emphasizes in his epistle (4:13-17), that is, seeking to know and practice the will of God in all our decisions.

The Danites Move

Then, on their favourable report (18:8-10), a large part of the tribe of Dan began the journey north to possess the country. Once again, they came by the house of Micah, with the result that they robbed him of his house of gods and took his Levite-priest with them. A mild remonstrance by the Levite (18:18) was all that came from him, and when he saw the prospect that they offered, he was glad (v. 20). It did not bother him to take part in stealing what actually belonged to Micah. He saw a greater position, more power and influence, and a better salary and went with alacrity to join them. It was a "better call," so off he went. This has been replicated many times in the practices of our religious world down to the present day, so we need not comment.

Of course, Micah protested but to no avail (18:22-24). They were too strong for him, so he had to bear the loss and keep silence. It may be that his loss was actually his gain, if it rid him of a house of idols!

Closing Observations

The chapter closes with the report of their success and their establishment in the land of their choosing. The passage draws our attention to several very important facts. The first, in Judges 18:30, tells us that the Levite-priest was Jonathon, the son of Gershom, the son of Manasseh (KJV). However, we know that the father of Gershom was Moses (Ex. 2:22; 18:3) and it seems clear from other translations and from respected scholars of the text, that this is what was meant. It seems possible that the thought of a grandson of Moses being thus involved was so revolting to the Masoretes (who were responsible to copy the Scriptures) that they made a change involving a small letter in the name. The idea that a grandson of Moses would be among the first of Israel to fall into idolatry was repulsive and abhorrent to their minds. It reminds us of the possibility that children of an illustrious father might be involved in departure from the Lord. No matter how great or spiritual a man might be, he cannot guarantee the faithfulness of his own family after him.

The second thing to note is that this spiritual evil continued until the day when they were taken captive. That could mean the day when this book was written, but possibly, it refers to what occurred in 2 Kings 15:29. This part of the nation was among the first to be taken into captivity and this statement shows that departure such as this is usually long-standing. One would judge that this form of idolatrous worship merged with Jeroboam's religion when he came to power. One of his altars was in Bethel but the other was placed in Dan (1 Kgs. 12:29). It is notable that in Bethel, Jeroboam had to place the priests that he had ordained (1 Kgs. 12:32) but there is no mention of those priests in Dan. Could it be that it was because there was a priesthood already in place as a result of what occurred in Judges 18? Possibly. There was little difference between the two forms of worship in these passages, so they likely formed his priesthood in that center.

The last observation is that this departure took place *"all the time that the house of God was in Shiloh"* (Judg. 18:31). This is the first mention of the term *"house of God"* in our Bibles after Genesis 28. It emphasizes that this was a rival "house of gods" but its existence was not because they lacked a proper place where they could worship. The tabernacle, the house of God at Shiloh, was the place that God had ordained for His people to gather and where they should have focused their spiritual attention (Deut. 12:5, 11, 14, 18, 21, 26). The existence of the house of God in Shiloh was a rebuke to their pretensions to have a proper center for worship.

This condition, seen at this point in the book, only emphasizes to us what has been a consistent point of departure in the church age. It is only another expression of the self-will of men, another example of men *"doing that which was right in their own eyes."* God never instituted many patterns of worship in one place, but we learn from His Word that His purpose is that one pattern should be duplicated in many places (1 Cor. 1:2; 4:17; 7:17; 14:37). In Israel there was to be only one place of worship and it is still God's mind that the assembly in a locality should be the gathering center for all His people. The assembly is an expression of the unity of the saints, representing the unity of the body as seen in that place. The assembly is not a miniature of the body of Christ, but the assembly should represent it in that locality. God's Word teaches this truth only, and anything else is a departure from it. May the Lord help us, with humbleness of spirit and acknowledgement of failure, to continue in that pattern until our days of service come to an end.

13

"Right in His Own Eyes"
Moral Degeneration and Fratricide

In the sad events that follow, once again a Levite in Mt. Ephraim is the central player. This one seems to have been a man who, though professedly serving the Lord, displayed indulgence of the flesh and personal desires. He was not forbidden to have a concubine, but that relationship was not quite the same as if she were indeed his wife. From his later attitude and acts toward her in Gibeah, it seems that she was only physically his without any genuine love for her (19:25). In addition, he was content to tarry with her father, eating, drinking and making merry for five days, so it seems that he was a man who could be easily persuaded to indulge the flesh. This characteristic, along with the evil acts done by the men of Gibeah, by the tribe of Benjamin and by the entire nation of Israel, expresses what happens when *every man did that which was right in his own eyes.*

The fact that the prominent man in this chapter, as in chapter 17, was a Levite, seems to indicate that there was a poor state among the leadership of God's people. These were men who were responsible to teach the law as well as serve in the tabernacle (Deut. 33:10). Therefore, their actions in these chapters suggest a breakdown in the quality of leadership among God's people that resulted in general failure of the nation. The character of the people was the result of the example and teaching that they had received. Since that leadership was at a low ebb, we cannot wonder at events that resulted. It is notable that there is no mention of the elders or oversight of the assembly in 1 Corinthians. One might wonder if they were either powerless to correct the evil that Paul addresses, or perhaps it indicates that they were involved in the evil. An assembly can never rise higher than those who have responsibility to lead the saints; thus, it is important that those men who have that responsibility manifest the highest spiritual character possible so that they will be able to exercise a godly influence to lead the assembly properly.

This corresponds with conditions of our day, a day that is near the coming of our Lord to close this church age. Indulgence of fleshly desires, even by men in religious circles, is all too common. Moral iniquity by leaders in the religious circle takes place all too readily. Others are quick to judge them, but also, due to the general weakness that prevails, very quick to pass over sin. The standard set by Samson in the previous chapters seemed to determine the moral tone of all that followed. As has already been noted, the moral practices of the nation were the logical result of their denying the Lord's authority. These conditions, sadly, result when men reject a divine standard for their behaviour and cast off God's sovereign control.

An Unsettled Levite

Exactly what initiated these sad events is not clear. We learn from Judges 19:1, that this Levite was *"sojourning on the side of mount Ephraim,"* so he seems to be like the Levite in chapter 17. He was not a man who occupied a particular sphere of service for God; he was not a man who was settled, and so he was wandering and sojourning.

In the assembly sphere, it is vital that believers have established themselves on the principles of an assembly, so that they are sure why they are there and what the Lord wants them to do. Convictions that we express by our full commitment to the place that God has chosen will preserve us from wandering wherever our desires might lead us. Those established convictions will also make us useful for the edification and blessing of the assembly where God has placed us.

Some believers never seem content in any local assembly; there is always something wrong in any place, and elements always exist that cause dissatisfaction in their hearts. As a result, they seem to move from one place to another, from one assembly to another assembly, looking for a "perfect" place, which, of course, they never can find. It is much better, and in harmony with God's Word, if believers recognize that no assembly is perfect, but that they can seek to help that company where God has put them through their example and service, if not by their instruction.

His Unfaithful Concubine

Exactly what his concubine's deed was is somewhat hard to determine accurately. The Authorized Version says that his concubine *"played the whore against him, and went away from him"* (19:2), indicating marital unfaithfulness on her part. However, Josephus and other translations of the passage (RSV, Moffatt, Latin Vulgate, and Septuagint) indicate that she was angry with him, or disgusted with his behaviour and returned to her father's house for this reason. There is some reason to consider that view, since if she were actually guilty of adultery against him, it would hardly follow that he would go after her to seek to bring her home as he did. Nevertheless, we can see that their relationship was not as it should have been, especially since he had the responsibility to lead God's people by his personal example of life. Paul instructs the saints regarding the character and life of an elder in 1 Timothy 3, and those standards, including his marital relationship, are of the highest level and should be maintained.

Their journey homeward, after his stay of five days in her father's house, led them by Jerusalem (v. 10), but he refused to stay there because it was not an Israelite city at that time. Perhaps he would have been more secure in that city than in Gibeah, the city that he chose. Events that took place in Gibeah repeated the characteristics of Sodom and Gomorrah. What a sad state, when a city of those who professed to be the people of God had sunk to such a level of depravity! It shows that even God's professed people, whether genuine or only in name, can display depths of sin and ruin if not genuinely converted and controlled by God's Spirit. What took place in that city caused the nation to respond, *"There was no such deed done nor seen from the day that the children of Israel came up out of the land of Egypt unto this day"* (19:30).

Paul said in 1 Corinthians 5:1 that the sin among those saints was *"such fornication as is not so much as named among the Gentiles,"* so we learn that this kind of evil behaviour can cause even God's enemies to blaspheme, as with David's sin (2 Sam. 12:14). One might wonder what the Jebusites of Jerusalem thought of these people when they heard and observed these events!

After what took place during that tragic night in Gibeah, we learn what the Levite did upon arriving home with her body. In his indignation, he cut her body into 12 pieces and sent it into all the coasts of Israel (19:29). One can understand the emotional reaction of anyone who has gone through a night like that; however, little did the Levite know what would result from what he did. The entire nation was stirred with an emotional response, desiring to execute retribution on those who had committed this terrible deed.

Mistakes Committed

Permit a few comments on the way in which the Levite handled this sad affair. Not everyone will agree with this assessment, but it is worth consideration. How did the Levite deal with this problem? First, he spread the sinful deed as widely as possible. Instead of approaching the elders and leaders of Gibeah first, he appealed to the entire nation of Israel. He spread the information about what the men of Gibeah had done to the far ends of the nation and stirred up all the people. Should he not have gone to the elders of Gibeah, and if that failed, then to the rulers of Benjamin? Only after all had failed should he have appealed to the entire nation. Is there not a principle that sin or problems among God's people should be dealt with on the local level first? Matthew 18:15-17 teaches us that if our brother sins, we are to go to him personally to seek to gain him. Only after we and others have made repeated efforts to settle the problem should it develop into a matter for the local assembly to deal with (certainly not a wider sphere than that).

Some teach that if an assembly fails to judge sin, then other assemblies of the surrounding area should deal with it. We have no Scripture for any other assembly interfering in the affairs of a local testimony! It should be a local matter and should be dealt with on that level.

One might say that the conditions in Gibeah had sunk so low that the Levite had no hope to receive justice in that city. However, it does not say that in the text! That may have been the case; nevertheless, he should have gone to them so that they could have exercised their responsibility to deal with this sinful act. His action undermined their authority as responsible leaders of that city. Had he done that, there could have been two possible results: one is that the elders of Gibeah might have been aroused to realize how bad conditions were in their city and they would then have had to deal with them. The other is that following that pattern might have preserved the nation from the general bloodshed that resulted. We can learn something about how we ought to deal with problems in a local setting from reading these chapters.

Not only did the Levite spread the problem to the entire nation, but he also did it in a very inflammatory manner; he divided her dead body with its bones and sent those parts into all the coasts of Israel (19:29). Saul did something very similar when he wanted to rouse Israel to fight against Nahash in 1 Samuel 11:7, but he hewed a yoke of oxen in pieces instead. That was acceptable, and it was for a worthy purpose so that the inhabitants of Jabesh-gilead would be saved. In this case, the Levite could not have chosen a more vivid manner to stir the emotions of any who viewed those parts of her corpse! What would anyone have thought when they saw those pieces of her mutilated body arrive? They would have, as was the case, responded with the highest degree of indignation and outrage. Is it possible that problems between saints or in a local assembly can be spread in a manner that incites an emotional reaction in those who hear of it? This can, and does, take place even without the hearers knowing all the related facts of the case. The Levite was, because of this manner of acting, partly responsible for the terrible events that resulted.

Basis of the Warfare

After hearing the Levite's report (20:4-7), all the tribes except for Benjamin moved to act. F. C. Jennings notes that in giving his account of the wickedness, he did it "with a natural care not to expose his own selfish baseness." First, before attempting to hear what the men of Gibeah or the tribe of Benjamin might say for themselves, they bound themselves with an oath to *"do... according to all the folly that **they** have wrought in Israel"* (20:10). Notice the fivefold repetition of "we will." Do we see any indication that they asked counsel of the Lord? Not, "we will do the Lord's will," or anything like that. They never waited on the Lord at this point to determine what was His will for them. It was their own will that they expressed when they selected 1/10th of the men of the tribes to bring their judgment on these men. Did they send men to Gibeah to remind the elders of that city of their responsibility? Did they inquire to learn exactly what had taken place? No. They simply decided to act and then determined what they would do. They were in a right position as they gathered, but their condition was deplorable.

More Mistakes Made

There are several mistakes here. One is that they should not have come together to the exclusion of Benjamin. They were like some in Corinth (1 Cor. 1:10-12) in that they formed their own groups and took a superior attitude to their brethren. Then, their mistake also lay, not only in failing to seek God's mind about what they should do, but also in the fact that they never judged themselves. As C. A. Coates puts it,

> "They did not feel it as the sin of Israel, but as the sin of Gibeah. If they had felt it as the sin of Israel, they would have all been on their faces before God, confessing it as their own sin. . . There was no sign of their being humbled before God. They did not seek direction; they decided what they would do. . . It was right, but they were not moving with God in it."

"All the ways of a man are clean in his own eyes; but the Lord weigheth the spirits" (Prov. 16:2). *"Every way of a man is right in his own eyes: but the Lord pondereth the hearts"* (Prov. 21:2). They failed to see that the same base possibilities resided in all of

them as well. They had never acted to judge what Micah had done in the previous chapters. Why this? If they were going to *"put away evil from Israel"* (20:13), they would have had to include all the tribes, for all had some measure of guilt in them. They could see wrong in another, but not in themselves. Is that not characteristic of human nature? We are all guilty of it to some extent, at least at some time in our lives.

We can see this in a personal reaction to a brother or sister when we hear what "they" have done. It can also be expressed in the hasty action of an assembly to judge evil (and rightly so, for it must be judged), but without self-judgment first taking place in all who are involved. We have instruction along this line in Galatians 6:1-2. The purpose of discipline is not the destruction of a brother or sister; it is the desire to *"restore such an one,"* and this can only be done by those who are spiritual and who consider themselves in the same light. Our Lord said, *"with what judgment ye judge, ye shall be judged"* (Matt. 7:1-2), so that the same standard of righteousness must be applied to ourselves as well as to the offender. Paul writes to the Corinthian saints with regard to sin in the assembly, *"Ye have not rather mourned, that he that hath done this deed might be taken away from among you"* (1 Cor. 5:2). If they had done so, even in the face of possible inability or unwillingness on the part of some to deal with that evil condition, God would certainly have come in to judge it, as took place in 1 Corinthians 11:30-32.

There is no doubt that Benjamin should have dealt with the evildoers. We cannot justify them either! However, the word of the tribes to Benjamin was *"what wickedness is this that is done among **you**?"* (20:12). That is to say, "This wickedness is among you, but we are free of it." Did they really expect that Benjamin would respond to that approach? Therefore, war between brethren ensued.

It is sad to note that Israel bound themselves under an oath that was foolishly taken. We saw a foolish oath in the case of Jephthah. This oath resulted in a compounding of their problem in the end (21:5, 7). It is as if they had determined from the first that this tribe would be exterminated from among them. Saul bound his people under a foolish oath in their warfare with the

Philistines in 2 Samuel 14, and that oath almost cost the life of Jonathan. Be careful what we swear or promise to do in this way; it may cause greater problems later in life. It may be possible to stand so rigidly on our "principles," that we only end up acting irrationally and unreasonably, with the result that we ultimately will compound the problem.

The First Battle

One might say that their first act expressed a right attitude in some respects. They came before the Lord to ask counsel (for the first time). However, notice that they never asked, "**Should** we go up to battle against Benjamin?" They never asked, "What should we do in this case and how can we bring about results that are according to God's will?" They asked with the assumption that they would go up to battle, and it is with "the children of Benjamin." At this point there was no mention of "Benjamin, my brother" (as in vv. 23, 28). The relationship was not foremost in their minds, so they acted with severity and cruelty toward them. The question of Judges 1:1 was with regard to who would go up first against the Canaanites to battle, and God selected Judah. It seems that Judah was again going out to battle (v. 18), but they were almost putting their brother, Benjamin, in the same class as their enemy. Only Judah should have been principally involved, for the concubine was from that tribe (19:1).

Numerically, the first day's battle was very lopsided: 400,000 men of Israel were against only 26,700 men of Benjamin. Therefore, it must have seemed strange to them that the results were weighted so much in Benjamin's favour with 22,000 men of Israel being destroyed. It is stranger that they only began to ask the Lord "Why?" at this point. They began to express some measure of exercise before God so that now, for the first time, they call Benjamin "my brother" (v. 23). They begin to manifest some tenderness of spirit as they think of the results from that first day. God was going to discipline the entire nation, not just a tribe or a city. It shows that when we presume to judge our brother without first judging ourselves, we may find that there will be a price to pay in personal loss that will humble us in the presence of God.

The Second Battle

Results from the second day of battle were not much different! Now 18,000 men were smitten by Benjamin. This resulted in the destruction of 40,000 men out of 400,000 men of Israel. They had spoken of 1/10th of Israel's men going to battle against Benjamin (20:10) and now 1/10th of those men have been destroyed. It was not Benjamin only that was being disciplined by God; His hand touched the entire nation so that it produced the remorse recorded in Judges 20:26.

We easily notice that there were two occasions when they expressed this degree of sorrow in God's presence. In Judges 21:2 they sense the great loss resulting from the near loss of an entire tribe of Israel. Losing 40,000 men first, then an entire tribe would cause deep sorrow and produce soul-searching, would it not? Why did they not react in this manner when they first heard of the sin in Gibeah? It seems that it takes an extreme expression of God's hand of discipline to produce the proper state of soul before Him! Prior to this moment, they were judging their brother from a position of assumed self-righteousness, and God could not be with them in it. At this point we learn that they wept, expressing the depth of their sorrow. Then they sat before the Lord, and this would make them sensitive to His voice and His will. They fasted, and denied themselves all that would naturally give them pleasure. Lastly, they offered burnt offerings and peace offerings before the Lord. One might wonder why there is no mention of a sin offering; we would think that this was surely the place for one! However, the burnt and peace offering expressed the ground of their acceptance before God and the expression of their fellowship with Him and one another. They represent Christ, as the One who has given us a perfect standing in God's presence, and through whom we have fellowship with Him and one another. On that ground, communion Godward and manward is very important and can be expressed. They had failed in all these expressions of exercise at the first, but now God's hand had brought them low. Expected success in their enterprise against Benjamin had resulted in defeat and loss. How contrary to what they had expected, but how consistent with the way by which God works to discipline His people. After having done all those things, they enquired of the Lord to seek His will.

For the first time, we read about Phinehas fulfilling his proper responsibility, representing Israel in their exercise before the Lord. He would likely be quite elderly at this point, since he was the high priest who had previously expressed God's assessment of their actions and who had judged sin in the camp for God (Num. 25:7). He had been involved in their warfare against the Midianites in Numbers 31:6. He was a militant priest, one who had a zeal for God and who would defend His honour. He represents a person in priestly capacity who knows how to judge sin in a godly way. God says about him, *He was zealous for my sake* [with my jealousy] *among them, that I consumed not the children of Israel in my jealousy*" (Num. 25:11). He would not have a vindictive attitude toward anyone of Israel; his viewpoint would be along the line of what was for God's honour and what was consistent with His will.

The mention of the ark at this point is a reminder that they were coming to the basis of their established unity as God's people. It was the expression of the faithfulness of God in their midst, even though they had been so unfaithful. In addition, for the first time, they considered the possibility that the Lord's will was for them to cease the warfare (Judg. 20:28). That was a good thought, in that they were willing to submit to whatever was the revealed will of God in the matter. This, of course, is absolutely essential in all matters of assembly discipline.

The Third Day

It seems significant that victory for them comes on the third day, but we leave the reader to consider its meaning. Now, using the stratagem of Israel when they defeated Ai (Josh. 8), they drew the children of Benjamin out of Gibeah where they easily overcame them. This time the Lord was on the side of Israel (20:35), and they destroyed the Benjaminites without any mercy (20:43-48). What they did was a sad contrast with God in His judgment; even in the execution of His anger He shows mercy (2 Sam. 24:16; Ps. 78:38; Isa. 40:2; 54:8; Joel 2:13-14). He, not they, should be the example for us.

It was good that six hundred men of Benjamin were able to escape the slaughter! They were much like Jotham in chapter 9, who escaped the fratricidal sword of his half-brother Abimelech. But, consider the extremity of their vengeance against their brother. They *"trode them down with ease"* (v. 43). They *"gleaned of them … five thousand men"* in the highways (v. 45). They *"pursued hard after them unto Gidom"* (v. 45). And they *"smote them with the edge of the sword, as well the men of every city, as the beast, and all that came to hand: also they set on fire all the cities that they came to"* (v. 48). It seems that they lost any semblance of reasonableness when they overcame their brethren. They were **cruel** to the extreme! No wonder, when we come to Judges 21:1-2, we read that they *"wept sore."* Well they might!

Are there any cases of extreme actions in assembly discipline? Are there not examples of brethren acting far more severely than is warranted? Is it not true, that in some cases a brother or sister has been put away from an assembly with no possibility of their ever returning? Discipline in an assembly is scripturally required, but we must, if we are to carry out God's mind in discipline, seek to act consistently and reasonably, being guided by the Scriptures. Joseph is an excellent example of a man who dealt properly with his own brethren to judge their sin but who also acted to restore fellowship (Gen. 42-45). Paul dealt with the believers in Corinth the same way regarding the sin that existed in the assembly (1 Cor. 5; 2 Cor. 2:4-10). It takes spiritual, godly men to properly judge sin when it appears among God's people so that the one being dealt with can be fully restored in the end, if possible. May God give us that discernment and consistency to act with righteousness as well as with mercy in these matters.

The Aftermath

Even after executing their vengeance on Benjamin and nearly eliminating that tribe, they expressed no repentance for what they had done, neither was there any indication of self-judgment as there should have been. "Israel in this last view we have of her here never confesses her true condition; and much it is to be feared that in this she will picture all too faithfully at

213

least one point in which the church will also woefully fail at the closing period of her testimony on earth" (F. C. Jennings). Self-judgment and honest confession of our own sinful condition is the hardest thing to do; far easier to judge our brethren than to judge ourselves!

Because of their foolish oath and their extreme severity with Benjamin, they had to face the dilemma of the near extermination of a tribe in Israel. Even as they offered burnt offerings and peace offerings to the Lord as an expression of their worship (21:4), they failed to seek His will to learn what they should do.

Once again they compounded the atrocity by deciding to enforce another of their oaths (notice how many times they did this) to put anyone to death who did not participate in their action against Benjamin. They balanced one foolish oath with another. They had decided to cut off anyone who had not agreed with their judgment, or who could not participate in their action. Since the men of Jabesh-gilead had not come to the battle, then they would eliminate them as well. "For the people will religiously keep their oaths! They must maintain their 'principles'! Their 'principles' demanded the extirpation of a tribe; and now the same strict 'principles' require the extirpation of a city to save that tribe from extirpation" (F. C. Jennings). They could not permit any of the nation to remain neutral, even if they might have had good reasons for refusing to participate; they must now pay the price for non-participation. Even though Israel was repenting of the severity of her action against Benjamin, their conscience seems to have been hardened so that they failed to recognize the injustice of this further action.

The absurdity of their vow to eliminate Jabesh-gilead is that their judgment on that city was selective and unrighteous in every aspect. The vow was that **all** would be killed, but they spared 400 unmarried virgins from that number. It was another case of them doing that which was right in their own eyes and not seeking the mind of God. Wrong principles result in inconsistency of their application, and some might be cut off and destroyed while others might be spared.

Those 400 were not enough to satisfy the need so that the tribal remnant of Benjamin could continue, so another expedient was selected in Judges 21:19-23. The first expedient involved murder, the second involved kidnapping! How strange man's ways can be when he is not subject to God's will nor actively seeking to know that will. Israel covered their self-righteous behaviour toward their brother Benjamin by their action, but the book closes with God's commentary on the entire affair. The statement apparently ends the book on a note of anxious anticipation for the day of established rule that was yet future. Israel must yet pass through the unsettled conditions under Samuel and the limited attempts of Saul (another who failed to submit to the will of God completely) until it would arrive at the glorious days of David and Solomon. The closing verse of this book seems to give a sense of that anticipation even as it reveals the underlying basis for the problems that Israel faced in these tumultuous times.

Do we learn from the pattern of Israel's behaviour during these days that we are much the same? We read that these things have been written for our admonition and learning (Rom. 15:4; 1 Cor. 10:11), so we should take heed and seek not to fail in the same way. The question is whether or not we are willing to learn from their sad history. It is so easy to apply this teaching to others, and, as a result, we fail to profit from it personally. The history of the church age, as we have attempted to show, has not been much different in principle, so we can easily apply this pattern to us so that we might learn from it and be preserved. Only as we recognize the same tendencies in ourselves and among us will we be preserved from making the same mistakes. May the Lord help us to do so as we live in the anticipation of His coming again and in view of our responsibility to our absent Lord Jesus Christ.

14

Conclusion

We have sought to trace the events God has recorded in this book and apply them to our lives personally as well as to the conduct and practices of assemblies. In harmony with the original premise of this book, we have noticed the correspondence between the major periods of the judges and the seven churches addressed by the Lord in Revelation 2-3. **The similarity is more than coincidental**; we recognize that the downward spiral of events in this historical book is typical of what the Lord presents in His letters to those churches. We see those letters present a prophetic view of the church age. As a result, we recognize that the Lord is giving us His assessment of the sequential conditions of the periods of church history and of the present systems in Christendom.

Since Judges presents an allegorical view of those churches and the words of the Lord in Revelation 2-3 address them directly, it is clear that the Lord is seeking to warn His people in order to preserve them. To ignore these warnings is our loss, since, as we have noticed already, *"whatsoever things were written aforetime were written for our learning"* (Rom. 15:4) and *"all these things happened unto them for ensamples* [types]: *and they are written for our admonition, upon whom the ends of the world are come"* (1 Cor. 10:11). We have their examples of failure to warn us, but we also have repeated examples of God's merciful restoration to encourage us.

How solemn to see that the events of these latter chapters are characteristic of the days that approach the end of this age; men thinking that they are doing right—and in their own eyes what they do is right—but rejecting divine authority at the same time. Is that not what prevails in our religious or secular world today? Does it not make us long for the establishment of the righteous kingdom of our God and Savior Jesus Christ? Yet, it is our responsibility as believers to acknowledge and submit to His authority in our lives today. The condition of others in an assembly or in the world is not the standard that should prevail in our lives. It is the King established upon the throne of our hearts that expresses His authority and gives His guidance to those who are submissive to Him. Peter admonished the saints, *"But sanctify the Lord God* [or "the Lord the Christ," or "Christ as Lord"] *in your hearts"* (1 Pet. 3:15).

We have a responsibility to live and act personally and collectively as those who gladly yield their obedience to Him and have crowned Him "Lord of all." His Word says that many will come to Him in that day saying, *"Lord, Lord..."* (Matt. 7:21), but those will not enter into the kingdom of heaven; those who **do** the will of His Father which is in heaven enter that kingdom, and they express it practically in their lives. Those who do so presently enjoy what God will fully express in the day of Christ's rule. They know the peace of God ruling (exercising control) in their hearts (Col. 3:15). They are filled with joy and praise and their lives are worthy of the Lord unto all pleasing (pleasing Him in all things) and they are *"fruitful in every good work and increasing in the knowledge of God"* (Col. 1:10).

We trust that the thoughts expressed on this practical and typical book will serve to cause every reader who is a believer in the Lord Jesus to seek to serve Him *"acceptably with reverence and godly fear"* (Heb. 12:28). It is our desire that in every sphere of our lives and service all might be *"to the praise of His glory"* (Eph. 1:3), and that He might be honoured as a result.

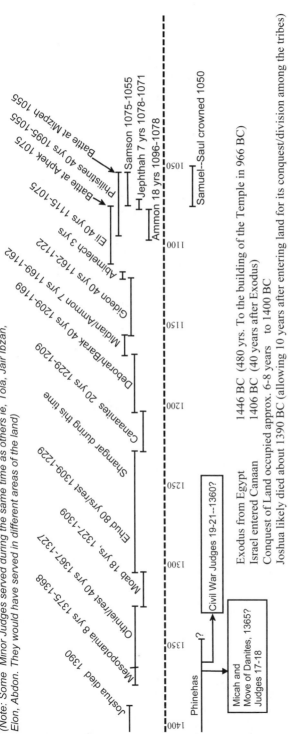

SUGGESTED CHRONOLOGY OF THE JUDGES

(Note: Some Minor Judges served during the same time as others ie, Tola, Jair Ibzan, Elon, Abdon. They would have served in different areas of the land)

Joshua died 1390

Mesopotamia 8 yrs 1375-1368

Othniel/rest 40 yrs 1367-1327

Moab 18 yrs 1367-1327

Ehud 80 yrs/rest 1309-1229

Shamgar during this time

Canaanites 20 yrs 1229-1209

Deborah/Barak 40 yrs 1209-1169

Midian/Ammon 7 yrs 1169-1162

Gideon 40 yrs 1162-1122

Abimelech 3 yrs

Eli 40 yrs 1115-1075

Ammon 18 yrs 1096-1078

Battle at Aphek 1075

Philistines 40 yrs 1095-1055

Battle at Mizpeh 1055

Samson 1075-1055

Jephthah 7 yrs 1078-1071

Samuel--Saul crowned 1050

Phinehas

Micah and Move of Danites, Judges 17-18 1365?

Civil War Judges 19-21--1360?

Exodus from Egypt   1446 BC (480 yrs. To the building of the Temple in 966 BC)
Israel entered Canaan   1406 BC (40 years after Exodus)
Conquest of Land occupied approx. 6-8 years to 1400 BC
Joshua likely died about 1390 BC (allowing 10 years after entering land for its conquest/division among the tribes)

Saul crowned as King 1050 BC (119 years prior to Jeroboam I)
Jeroboam I as King   931 BC

Josiah's Passover   620 BC

**Dates and chronology according to Dr. Leon Wood, "Distressing Days of the Judges," Zondervan, 1975

219

Bibliography

Brown, Driver, Briggs, <u>Hebrew and English Lexicon of the Old Testament</u>. Oxford, England: Clarendon Press, 1980.

Coates, C. A., <u>An Outline of Joshua, Judges, and Ruth</u>, England: Stow Hill Bible and Tract Depot.

Fausset, A. R., <u>Fausset's Bible Dictionary</u>.

Gooding, A. M. S., <u>The Thirteen Judges</u>. Glasgow, Scotland: Gospel Tract Publications, 1986.

Grant, F.W., <u>The Numerical Bible</u>. New York, NY: Loizeaux Brothers, 1932.

Jackson, J. B., <u>A Dictionary of Scripture Proper Names</u>. Neptune, NJ: Loizeaux Brothers, 1974.

Jamieson, Fausset, and Brown, <u>Commentary on the Whole Bible</u>. Grand Rapids, MI: Zondervan Publishing House, 1973.

Jennings, F.C., <u>Judges and Ruth</u>. Northumberland, England: Central Bible Hammond Trust.

Keil, C. F. and Delitzsch, F., <u>Commentary on the Old Testament</u>. Peabody, MS: Hendrickson Publishers, 1996.

Miller, Andrew, <u>Miller's Church History</u>. Addison, IL: Bible Truth Publishers, 1980.

Ridout, Samuel, <u>How to Study the Bible</u>.

Ridout, Samuel, <u>Judges and Ruth</u>.

Smith, W., <u>Smith's Bible Dictionary</u>.

Tozer, A. W., "God Tells the Man Who Cares," <u>The Best of A. W. Tozer</u>. Grand Rapids, MI: Baker Book House, 1978.

Vine, W. E., <u>Expository Dictionary of New Testament Words</u>. 1940.

Wood, Leon, <u>Distressing Days of the Judges</u>. Grand Rapids, MI: Zondervan Publishing House, 1975.

by
Joel Portman

THE
Holy Spirit

A Consideration
of His Person and work
toward the Believer
and in the
Local Assembly

The Holy Spirit, With You and In You
Joel Portman
Item #: X-HS
A Consideration of the Holy Spirit's Person and work toward
the Believer and in the Local Assembly. In a day filled with
religious confusion, this book should help the reader consider
and appreciate the work the Spirit is doing today.

GOSPEL FOLIO PRESS
I WILL PUBLISH THE NAME OF THE LORD

304 Killaly St. West | Port Colborne | ON | L3K 6A6 | Canada
1 800 952 2382 | E-mail: info@gospelfolio.com | www.gospelfolio.com

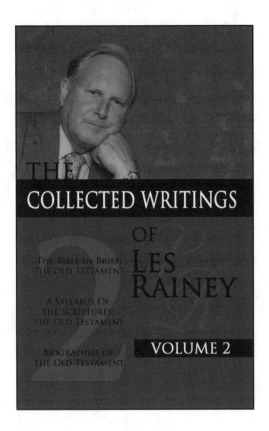

The Collected Writings of Les Rainey: Volume 2
Les Rainey
Item #: B-7309
This volume includes three books:
The Bible in Brief: The Old Testament,
A Syllabus of the Scriptures: The Old Testament, and
Biographies of the Old Testament.

GOSPEL FOLIO PRESS
I WILL PUBLISH THE NAME OF THE LORD

304 Killaly St. West | Port Colborne | ON | L3K 6A6 | Canada
1 800 952 2382 | E-mail: info@gospelfolio.com | www.gospelfolio.com

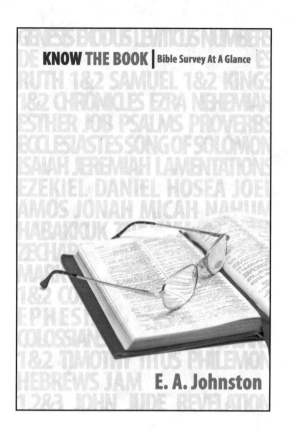

Know the Book

E. A. Johnston

Item #: B-7337

A survey of each book of the Bible. At a glance the reader can grasp the central truths and content of each book. It is a helpful extra tool for Bible study or teaching.

GOSPEL FOLIO PRESS

I WILL PUBLISH THE NAME OF THE LORD

304 Killaly St. West | Port Colborne | ON | L3K 6A6 | Canada
1 800 952 2382 | E-mail: info@gospelfolio.com | www.gospelfolio.com